THE BEST OF TIMES

Growing up in Britain in the 1950s

Alison Pressley

Picture Acknowledgements:
Lilian Ream Exhibition Gallery:
p.19: *top right;* p.27: *top right;* p. 29; p. 52; p. 54; p. 75;

Front Cover:
Top: Advertising Archives
Bottom left: Dorling Kindersley Ltd.
Sooty puppet: Collector's World, London
Sooty Xylophone: David Huxtable "Old Advertising", London
Oxydol Box: David Huxtable "Old Advertising", London
Record Sleeve: Radio Days, London
Fabric: Radio Days, London
Chair: Arne Jacobson Swan Chair, Fritz Hansen™
Bush Radio: The Vintage Wireless Museum

The publisher would like to thank the author and the author's friends for the loan of personal
photographs, and apologizes if the name of any contributor has inadvertently been omitted.

Alison Pressley is a book editor, writer and publisher. She was born in 1947 in South Shields,
County Durham and was educated at South Shields Grammar Technical School for Girls,
Kingsbury County Grammar School and Manchester University, where she gained a BA in
American Studies in 1969. She left England in 1973 to travel the world via the hippie trail,
and has lived in Sydney, Australia since 1974. She has had work published by William Collins
(an adaptation of *Pregnant While You Work,* 1985) and Reader's Digest (*Why in the World?*
1993), and is currently publisher of a list of non-fiction books with Hodder Headline
Australia.

First published in Great Britain in 1999 by
Michael O'Mara Books Limited
9 Lion Yard
Tremadoc Road
London SW4 7NQ

A CIP catalogue record for this book is available from the British Library

ISBN 1-85479-458-2

 7 9 10 8 6

Edited by Yvonne Deutch
Designed by Design 23

Printed and bound in Singapore by Tien Wah Press

For Ma, Pa, Smithy and Cecil – the people who made the fifties the best of times for me

Acknowledgements

It will be fairly obvious to even the most casual reader of this book that it is based purely on personal recollections of the fifties. I have left historical research into statistics and hard facts to more formal and better qualified chroniclers. The idea of *The Best of Times* is to use people's memories – incomplete and flawed though they sometimes are – to build a picture of the decade through the eyes of its children. I hope that the experiences described in these pages strike many chords with readers. My main debt is to author Helen Townsend, whose book *Baby Boomers: Growing Up in Australia in the 1940s, 50s and 60s* (Simon & Schuster Australia, 1988) provided the idea, the inspiration and the role model. I would also like to thank all the friends and relatives whose reminiscences make up the bulk of the text: Joyce Foley, Peter Garland, Neal Gordon, Valerie Grove, Cliff Hall, Lisa Highton, Roy Jackson, Pat Kirby, Ray Kirby, Heather McCauley, Janet Prescott, Jennifer Roberts, Tony Roberts, Rosalind Snaith and Judy Spittlehouse. They all submitted to my video camera with great good humour and made compiling this book enormous fun.

Thanks are due to Carol Dix for allowing me to quote from her book *Say I'm Sorry to Mother* (Pan Macmillan, 1979), and to my sister Valerie Grove for leaning on her famous friends to provide reminiscences which appear throughout the book as *'My Fifties'*. Thank you also to those famous friends! A special thank you is due to Lisa Highton, without whose help the book would have languished in a drawer.

Finally, a huge thank you to Lesley O'Mara, Gabrielle Mander and Yvonne Deutch of Michael O'Mara Books for bringing the whole project to life.

ALISON PRESSLEY

We'll talk of sunshine and of song,
And summer days, when we were young;
Sweet childish days, that were as long
As twenty days are now.

WILLIAM WORDSWORTH, *TO A BUTTERFLY*, APRIL 1802

Foreword

You are amazed that the newsagent, who is aged about 27, cannot tot up the cost of three items, totalling one pound twenty, without a calculator. You remember having to calculate in your head how much a dozen eggs at twopence-three-farthings would cost. You remember farthings. You remember Liberty bodices, suspender belts, nylons, roll-on girdles, paper-nylon petticoats, winkle-picker shoes, crisps packets with little blue waxed paper twists of salt inside, Duffel coats, black Bakelite telephones with exchange names and simple numbers, the single plug-in wireless set shared by the entire family, the black Ford Popular car, the first 14-inch television screen around which the entire neighbourhood gathered to watch the Coronation, the first portable transistor radios.

You read the *Beano*, the *Eagle* and *Girl*. You remember Suez. You benefited from the Butler Education Act. You sat in rows of desks with lift-up lids and ink-wells. Your history classes were about kings and queens, your geography about capitals and the jute trade. Nobody mentioned global warming or the threat to the ozone layer; the only anxiety was the bomb – which could be banned, if you marched and sang loudly at the end of the decade. You went to the pictures on Saturdays. You bought 78 rpm records of Elvis Presley and Buddy Holly.

You are a Baby Boomer, born after World War II ended, just in time to enjoy the innocent, secure, never-had-it-so-good fifties. You had a really fab time at your twenty-first birthday in the swinging promiscuous sixties . . . You hit your fiftieth birthday in the nineties . . . and the Millennium finds you still in your prime . . .

VALERIE GROVE

Introduction

We were born into an innocent, optimistic world. Our parents had survived the horrors of World War II; the returning heroes, our fathers, came home to a world full of promise of better times to come. They were reunited with welcoming, lonely wives, and in a spirit of celebration and thanksgiving they conceived us – in unprecedented millions. We were the Baby Boomers, the fruits of joy after long separation. It was an auspicious beginning.

We were born in the years after the war, as Britain picked herself up, shook herself down and started all over again. In this world there was hardship, of sorts – but nothing like the Depression our parents and grandparents had endured. Rationing and shortages, to be sure, but also relative luxury: peace, and growing prosperity. Our world was one of trust, and neighbourly concern. We played innocently in the streets and parks of our neighbourhood, unmindful of the dangers that lurk today. They didn't exist, then.

We benefited from the Butler Education Act of 1944 and the construction of a 'Welfare State' in the late 1940s, and grew into the healthiest and most widely educated generation ever. Our early childhood was by today's standards austere, but by history's standards it was full of largesse. We thrived and prospered under the post-war expansiveness, and when we reached our teens towards the end of the fifties and the beginning of the sixties, we exploded. We became this – and perhaps, to date, any – century's most influential generation. The 'Swinging Sixties' still reverberate, still make waves. Its leaders still lead – although we are growing rather long in the tooth. The generations after us are beginning to resent us and our lingering influence: 'Move over', they say, 'let us have our day.'

So, before we are swamped forever by the tidal wave of generations now happening and to come, let's have one more celebration of us, the lucky generation who grew up in the best of times, in the best of places. Mindful of the second half of the quotation that serves as the title of this book (Dickens's 'It was the best of times, it was the worst of times' which opens *A Tale of Two Cities*), it is here acknowledged that our childhood wasn't perfect – but it was as close to perfect as it gets. Here's a toast to the fifties – the decade that made us – and everything it brought, from the Woodentops to Elvis, from Liberty bodices to blue suede shoes.

Contents

'Are you sitting comfortably?

Then I'll begin...'

PART 1
Living with Mother

Daily life at home

In the fifties, just about every pre-school child in Britain stayed home with either their mother or an aunt or grandmother during the day. Hardly any mothers went out to work, so the daily minutiae of the household – cleaning, cooking, shopping, tradesmen, neighbours – was as much a part of our early lives as it was a part of our mothers' lives. By today's standards, houses were cold, uncomfortable and fairly spartan: at the beginning of the decade such things as refrigerators and television sets were unknown in the average house. Few households had cars, so the shopping was done locally, with rare trips into town or a nearby city, and tradesmen – including grocers and greengrocers – would come to your door. For us, as children, the life of the immediate neighbourhood loomed large.

Housework and household style

In retrospect the fifties heralded the new modernism in interior décor and household style – it was, after all, the decade that saw the unprecedented spread of washing machines, refrigerators and vacuum cleaners. But reality, for most of us, was a house that was a relic of the pre-war days: dark, unbelievably cold, and with primitive plumbing arrangements.

Housework in the fifties followed a rigid time-table, regardless of the weather or anything else. Mondays were washdays. Tuesdays, ironing. Dusting and polishing were always done on Thursdays, the big shop on Fridays. Nothing whatsoever was done on Sundays – except, of course, vast amounts of cooking and washing up.

The sound of the vacuum cleaner was so depressing. As was the sight of my mother in her turban and pinny. She spent all day cleaning on Thursdays. Our furniture was all 'utility' furniture, very plain: square tables and armchairs, of no distinction.

After the weekly wash was done on Monday morning it would as likely as not rain, so the dining room would be filled with clothes horses draped in wet washing, completely obscuring the gas fire. The clothes would steam gently and we would sit frozen behind them. I hated wet Mondays.

Everybody did everything in the room where the fire was, in the winter. That was the only room that was halfway warm, except for at Christmas maybe. Going to the toilet was agony, it meant going out into the rest of the house, where it was always freezing.

Every room in our house was so cold. The kitchen with the range was the only really warm room; everywhere else had lino-covered floors, with the occasional rug, and a runner in the hall. It was like living in the Arctic Circle.

Our front room was never used. It was kept pristine and only used on formal occasions, which was hardly ever. It seems crazy now, the house was so small. We all sat crammed into the kitchen. But that was the way, then.

I remember going to my grandmother's house and noticing how quiet everything was. You could hear the clocks ticking, and papers rustling. I seemed to spend a lot of my childhood waiting for things to happen, and hearing quiet things: clocks ticking, birds singing. You couldn't go down and watch television if you woke up before the grown-ups, like kids can now.

Cousin Jill
(she's twice removed)
was (for spending)
thrice reproved

Hubby now no longer raving
Blesses her and Co-op saving!

...keep them lovely with RINSO washing!

RINSO will keep that jacket so soft and cuddly and help look after its pretty colour, too.

RINSO will keep the beauty of delicate smocking on that pretty nightdress and help keep all baby's things looking spruce and lovely!

RINSO treats those gay bright stripes with the care they deserve so they'll stay gay for a long long time.

Nighties are going gay — fascinating frills or sweet simplicity, in colourful fabrics. You'll feel lovely in them — and look it, too. But remember, gay fabrics need careful washing to keep them gay. So use Rinso always. Its rich, safe lather treats every washable fabric with such respectful care... really makes your pretty things last longer!

Rinso

will help KEEP those lovely things lovely longer!

We used to love going to our grandmother's house. She had a washhouse in the garden with a huge tub and a poss stick or plodger and a dolly blue and a washboard. It also had a dartboard, so invariably one of us would end up with a dart in our leg.

You've finished your wash— but is it only half done?

However well you wash your clothes, the final results still depend on the wringing. And only Acme wringing makes it certain that washday after washday your clothes will be as clean, crisp and sparkling as ever you could desire. Five million women already know this. Whether they use a washing machine, sink or tub, they all say . . . .

However you wash— you should have ACME wringing

ACME WRINGERS LIMITED DAVID STREET GLASGOW SE

Washing clothes was very labour intensive. Everything was washed in the one sink – kids, dishes, clothes. Mum did a clothes wash every day, without any mechanical assistance. The only piece of machinery was a mangle, a wringer. I tried very hard to put my fingers in it, and of course succeeded eventually.

Our weekly wash was done in the scullery, with a washboard and a mangle. The clothes were then hung outside on a clothes line, with a huge clothes prop to hold the line up. We didn't get a washing machine until the sixties.

Having a bath was such torture in winter, when anything out of the water froze, especially your back. And there wasn't that much water in the tank, either. Sunday night was bath night, so we'd have this terrible fire blazing all through the day on Sundays in summer, so that we could have a bath in the evening. It was hell.

Friday nights were bath night, and the tin bath would be brought in from the outside and filled with kettles of water. You had to get out of the tub on the coal fire side, because if you got out on the non-fire side you would simply die of cold.

My first baths were taken in the kitchen sink. It was a big, deep porcelain sink, as they all were then. Later on, when I was about four, we got a tin tub we used to keep out in the yard and pull in on bath nights.

Wash day is child's play!

It's goodbye to those wash day blues when you wash with one of Mr. Therm's NEW WASHING MACHINES! No hot water worries—Mr. Therm sees to that! The water is heated by Gas in the machine. You can have it boiling if you like! Then it's power agitated—and the washing's over in no time! Quiet, economical, efficient—thanks to Mr. Therm. See the latest Gas-heated washing machines at your Gas Showrooms—they're all on the easiest possible terms

Mr THERM burns to serve you

SIMON HOGGART
(B. 1946)

My Fifties

Scratchy grey flannel shorts and long socks with a ruler pushed down the right leg. Party telephone lines, so you could eavesdrop on neighbours' conversations. Never enough sweets because of rationing. Ford Consuls and Zephyrs – the first cars whose boots stuck out as far as their engines. AA patrolmen saluting. Cars whose suspension made you sick after twenty miles.

We had a dark, dank cellar where we kept our coal, and we used to keep our eggs in there too, in this great big china bowl, really huge – to me it looked like a small swimming pool – and the eggs were kept in this stuff called isinglass. I mean, now you just put them in the fridge, but we had to go down into this damp, dark cellar and put them in this liquid stuff. I used to think it was weird even then.

Part of the 'baby with the bath water' modernization of the fifties was people getting rid of their pianos. They would pay people to come and chop them up and take them away. I remember thinking at the time how awful this was. China went out, too – lots of really nice things. If you had a really nice old panelled door, you had to put hardboard over it, with beading all around. Same with fireplaces. Then you'd invite people in to come and look at the desecration. It was a real status symbol.

I remember those long, deep, cold stone sinks, scullery-type sinks with horrible bits of curtain under them, and cold stone floors. So some of the new fifties things were in fact improvements – warmer lino on the floor, nice new aluminium sinks and so on. But fifties kitchens were still really primitive. Hideous formica, and spiky-legged tables and things.

From the age of three until the age of nine – from 1950 to 1956 – I shared a room with my grandmother. I slept in a cot. My parents and my great-grandfather slept in two other rooms in the house, and we all lived in the only other room, the back kitchen. After that, we got a council house and I had a room to myself.

We used to keep our coal in the cupboard under the stairs. You'd take the coal-scuttle and use a big scoop to fill it with coal. One day when I went to fetch the coal there was an enormous toad sitting on top of the pile. I nearly screamed the house down.

I had to have a bath twice a week, which I thought was a bit of an imposition, with Lifebuoy soap which had a picture of a boy's face on it briefly before it turned into a hideous slimy sludge. Every other night had to be a DGW, which meant a Damned Good Wash. My mother would check me, and if I didn't pass inspection she would just dip the flannel – which was pretty rough – into the now-cold water and scrub vigorously behind my ears and neck and so on. I do it now to my own children, despite their cries of 'Mummy, don't!' Because you just see a child as some kind of wall with dirty marks on it.

We had a stone shelf in the pantry, and a meat safe with wire mesh over the front. Things didn't keep very long in the summer, though, so my mother would shop just about every day for perishables.

We had a pantry with an opening to the outside, covered in a sort of grille. Everything was kept on the shelves in that. It kept food pretty well, really. But Mummy still went shopping every day – twice a day, sometimes. And my sister and I would have to run errands all the time, when we were old enough. Most perishable food was bought on a daily basis. Tiny amounts. My uncle had a greengrocer's shop and he used to sell half an onion, or one apple, quite regularly.

As a very young child I was terrified of the woollen army blanket that covered my bed. They were the only bedclothes available after the war, but they were scratchy and grey – totally alien and threatening.

Progress in the Home

Hoover Limited take pride in the fact that their products are saving millions of housewives from hard, wearisome drudgery — not only in Britain but throughout the world. Wherever the name Hoover appears it is a guarantee of excellence.

THE WORLD-FAMOUS HOOVER CLEANER

The Hoover Cleaner, with its famous triple-action principle — " It beats . . . as it sweeps . . . as it cleans " — is undeniably the world's best cleaner — best in design, best in materials, best in quality of workmanship. T... is a model suitable for every size and type of home.

THE MARVELLOUS HOOVER ELECTRIC WASHING MACHIN...

The Hoover Electric Washing Machine has completely revolutionised the whole conception of washing-day in the home. It does the full weekly wash for a large family and yet is such a handy size—suitable for even the smallest kitchen.

VISIT THE HOOVER FACTORY

Visitors to the Festival of Britain are cordially invited to make a tour of the Hoover Factories at Perivale, Middlesex, or Merthyr Tydfil, South Wales, or Cambuslang, Scotland. Please write to, Hoover Limited, Perivale, or 'phone Perivale 3311 for more information.

HOOVER LIMITED

Factories at :
PERIVALE, MIDDLESEX · MERTHYR TYDFIL · HIGH WYCOMBE · CAMBUSLANG, SCOTLAND

Yes—but have you tried ZAL PINE FRESHNESS in your home?

You simply *must*! ZAL's the disinfectant with *all* the advantages you look for. It kills the germs without staining or harming anything. It leaves quite the most delightful pine smell. And it is a *treasure* of economy at only 1/- a bottle.

1/- a bottle
Extra large size 1/6

ZAL PINE FLUID DISINFECTANT

An Izal Product, backed by 60 years' experience of disinfectant manufacture

---

We had featherdown mattresses and quilts, and featherdown pillows; god knows what they did to your back, but they were immensely cosy to snuggle into.

I remember when a fitted carpet was installed, it seemed so modern. And when our first fridge arrived, and when we stopped having a plug-in radio. When our Electrolux vacuum cleaner arrived, long snaky thing, it was the last word in contemporary style.

Toilet paper in the fifties was revolting. We used stuff called Izal Germicide, which had the consistency – and the absorbency – of tracing paper, and smelt disgusting even before you'd used it. It came it nasty little cardboard boxes which took ages to fit into the metal holder, and each leaf was separate. You had to use at least half a dozen leaves to approximate a mass that would absorb any moisture at all – never mind anything else.

Mealtimes

Parents just after the war made sure that their children were well-nourished – almost too well-nourished – so they'd weigh up well at their next visit to the clinic. So families ate four meals a day, consisting of a cooked breakfast and a cooked meal at lunchtime, for many the main meal of the day and often called 'dinner'; then there'd be afternoon or 'high' tea, then supper.

We had bread fried in lard or dripping, which we called 'dip bread', for breakfast. It had to be really greasy before we were satisfied. I remember my sister saying scathingly 'Some people call this dip bread!' at a particularly dry piece she was given. It's a wonder we didn't die of heart failure at the age of eight.

It was terribly important to my mother that we always had a cooked, three-course breakfast: cereal, then bacon and eggs, then toast. Today it would be a killer, but at the time it seemed desperately important.

I was constantly made to drink an egg-in-milk – a cup of milk with an egg broken into it, whisked up – because it was supposed to be good for me. I thought, 'I hate this, I can't drink it', but I had to.

The packets of cornflakes we had for breakfast sometimes had little plastic gizmos in the bottom. I remember one was a little submarine you put baking powder in, and it went down and came up again. It really worked.

'Snap, crackle, pop' was a harbinger of the new order of things. New cereals, new advertising. Ready Brek was another.

My Mummy says...
"CARNATION has DOUBLE RICHNESS!"

"Feeling Peckish? You'll enjoy
PECK'S PASTES"
fish or meat equally delicious

Give them a PECK'S
"Quick Snack"   for a change

QUICK KIPPER CAKES. Mix together
1 large cupful mashed potato, 1 table-
spoon flour, ½ of jar Peck's Kipper Paste,
tablespoonful chopped parsley, a little salt,
a shake of pepper. Bind with beaten
egg: don't make too soft. Turn
on to floured board, roll to ⅛ in.
thickness, cut into rounds. Coat
with egg and breadcrumbs and deep
fry, or cook without coating in
greased frying-pan.

FOR PECK'S 'QUICK SNACK' RECIPES
IN NEW LEAFLET, WRITE TO HARRY PECK & CO. LTD., 20, DEVONSHIRE GROVE, LONDON, S.E.15

We used to walk home from school every lunchtime to have a meal, which we called 'dinner'. I remember standing at the back door and sniffing hard. If I could smell mince and potato – which I often could – I would refuse to enter the house.

The highlight of coming home from the swimming baths after the Splash Club on (usually freezing) Thursday nights was stopping off at the fish and chip shop for four penn'orth of fish and chips – with the *piece de resistance*, extra batter bits from the fish pan.

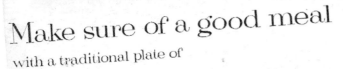

I had school dinners from day one because they were very cheap, but the food wasn't up to much. It was brought to the school in huge steel containers, so it was already congealed. The supervisor insisted that everyone clean their plates, and we had a dreadful piece of meat every day, full of fat and gristle, although I suppose that was all there was, after the war. She would look under the tables and everything, determined that every child should eat every morsel. So when I was about six I devised a clever system. I took two handkerchiefs to school each day. One was for blowing my nose, and the other was for taking the meat scraps home and dumping them in the bin.

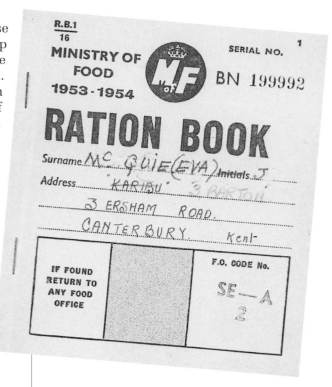

School dinners were terrible. It took me years before I could eat cabbage after I left school, because when they took the lid off the stainless steel containers the smell of the cabbage was nauseating.

I was always envious of my friend up the road because she had supper, which consisted of a packet of crisps and a mug of Ovaltine. We had a cup of hot milk which I hated, not because of the taste but because of the vile skin that would always form on the top. You could blow it away to the other side of the cup but you always ended up getting some in your mouth. Ugh!

MAUREEN LIPMAN
(B.1946)

My Fifties

My crayons were kept in a mauve tin of Ostermilk. My hair was permed with Twink. My brother had an elasticated belt of red and green stripes with a snake clip. I didn't. I had a checked dress with smocking and puffed sleeves. He had Meccano and knew how long a furlong was. I had cut-out dolls from the back of *Bunty* and boxes full of cut-out clothes. He could make a face like the Mekon in the *Eagle*, which terrified me. We played out in the 'Tenfoot' until teatime, which was Heinz spaghetti on toast or an egg cooked in a saucer in the oven and called, imaginatively, 'saucer egg'. The TV, when it arrived, was a Bush 12-inch. Dad bought us a Dansette record player and three records: Edmundo Ros, David Whitfield and 'Itsy Bitsy Teeny Weeny Yellow Polka Dot Bikini'. Vimto was my tipple in the break at Muriel Riley's Ballroom Dancing Classes where I led Bernice Segal round the floor in a neat Valeta. Forty years later I still try to lead. In times of extreme stress I still resort to Heinz tomato soup and a slice of sliced white.

We seemed to eat an awful lot of jam. My father would make plum jam, blackcurrant jam. We had a big garden with lots of vegetables and fruit trees. He'd bottle a lot of fruit, too.

When I visited my childless aunt and uncle for afternoon tea we would have either fish paste sandwiches, cut into triangles, or salmon paste sandwiches, or pink salmon sandwiches, followed by Libby's fruit salad with Carnation milk. I still remember swishing the Carnation milk around the fruit salad, and getting that little grape – because we didn't have that much fruit then, other than apples. Even oranges and bananas weren't that prevalent. And of course it was all strictly seasonal.

We always walked home for lunch, nobody stayed at school for lunch unless there was something wrong with them, because why wasn't their mother at home looking after them?

Food in our house was an absolute ritual. If you asked me what I had for dinner on the first Monday in 1950 and the last Friday in 1959, I would be able to tell you. Because Sunday was a beef joint, with a monumental, plate-sized Yorkshire pudding filled to the brim with gravy; Monday was cold beef, and Tuesday was beef stew. Wednesday was sausages and mash; Thursday was rabbit pie; Friday was fish – and I can't face fish now because of all those Friday dinners – and Saturday was sandwiches, eaten on the run before the football match or the cricket.

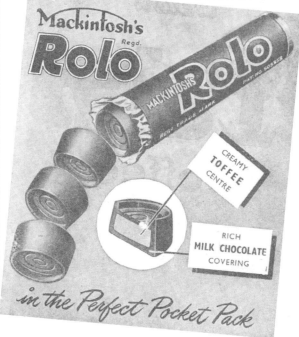

"Shh! Stop Tommy! I think Mummy's coming up with our OXO."

OXO

FOR A TASTY AND NOURISHING HOT DRINK

ENJOY THE STIMULATING PROPERTIES OF PRIME BEEF

Throughout the entire fifties we had only one meal: mince and mashed potatoes, with stewed apple and custard for pudding. We never went out to eat, and when we went on outings we took sandwiches made with bloater paste or Spam, and sometimes one of those fruit pies in cardboard boxes.

People used to mix butter and sugar together as a substitute for cream, which you just couldn't get unless you paid a fortune. It was called buttercream, I think. I never liked butter so I thought it tasted revolting.

Our grandmother used to churn her own butter. It was very scarce in those days, so she'd buy milk and churn it forever until she had butter. She was quite resourceful.

I remember lots of bulky foods. My favourite pudding was Spotted Dick, with lots of that revolting golden syrup, or treacle or custard. Of course it was just flour and water with a few raisins bunged in, boiled up in an old stocking or something. We always had plenty of rice puddings, because my Dad was the caretaker in a school and not all the kids drank their school milk, so we got all the leftover bottles.

We had terrible desserts, like rice pudding, tapioca, semolina. I hated all of them. Summer was all right, when we ate the fruit from our own trees, but winter was awful. Just like school dinners.

Our mother, like all mothers then, made a lot of cakes. We used to hang around the kitchen waiting until the mix was in the oven, then we could spoon and lick the mixing bowl clean. The taste of the mix was glorious, no matter what the type of cake, but neither my sister nor I cared for the cakes themselves. We always claimed they were 'just crumbs stuck together'.

I had a much older brother who was also of an age to be at the pub instead of home in time to eat the Sunday lunch. So there was always some recalcitrant male not doing his duty.

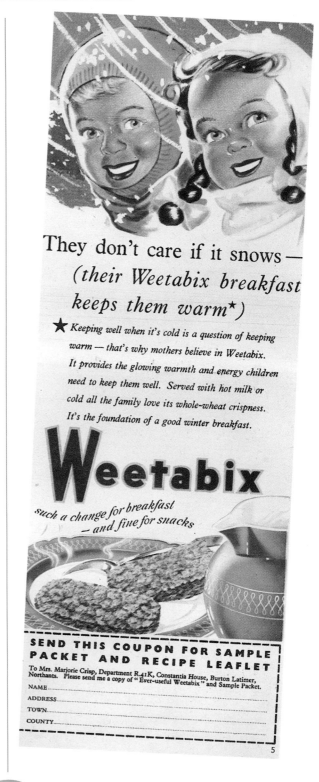

They don't care if it snows — (their Weetabix breakfast keeps them warm★)

★ Keeping well when it's cold is a question of keeping warm — that's why mothers believe in Weetabix. It provides the glowing warmth and energy children need to keep them well. Served with hot milk or cold all the family love its whole-wheat crispness. It's the foundation of a good winter breakfast.

Weetabix

such a change for breakfast — and fine for snacks

SEND THIS COUPON FOR SAMPLE PACKET AND RECIPE LEAFLET

To Mrs. Marjorie Crisp, Department R.41K, Constantia House, Burton Latimer, Northants. Please send me a copy of "Ever-useful Weetabix" and Sample Packet.

NAME...

ADDRESS...

TOWN..

COUNTY...

5

The drama would start early every Sunday morning. We'd get up and listen to Jean Metcalfe and Cliff Michelmore in 'Forces Favourites', which was as much a part of the Sunday ritual as having to peel potatoes and do sprouts and carrots.

We measured the Sunday cooking by what was on the radio. 'The Billy Cotton Band Show', 'The Navy Lark', 'Movie Go-Round'.

Vegetables seemed to go on for at least an hour. A lot of pea-shelling happened, then the peas were killed by overcooking like everything else.

Roast lamb had to be accompanied by mint sauce. I was in charge of collecting the mint from the garden and making the sauce, which consisted of equal parts of mint, sugar and brown vinegar, with a little bit of boiled water but not much. There was always a good slurpy bit down the bottom.

On Fridays we had real fish: kippers, and haddock poached in milk. To this day, I think things poached in milk look like someone's already eaten them.

Puddings involved cooking: Queen's pudding, angel cakes, rice pudding, caramel pudding, semolina. I could throw up at the thought of them.

When we were bought a packet of crisps — a rare treat — the real excitement was finding how many salts you had. Salt came in a twist of blue waxed paper, supposedly one per packet of crisps, but occasionally you'd get a windfall of three or even more twists of salt. And of course you had to use the lot, so if you did get the jackpot you'd end up with almost inedible crisps, slathered in salt.

Rationing was a great excuse for mothers. Whenever you wanted sweeties — just about every shopping trip — back would come the dreaded words, 'We haven't enough coupons left.' Nothing you could do about that, no matter what sneaking suspicions of perfidy lurked in your mind.

I remember the sweetie ration book, which was very real, and the day rationing was removed and I was able to go and buy a Mars bar. I got tuppence a week to spend on sweeties. All the sweeties in the sweetie shops were in jars, and you could get an awful lot of combinations for your money. You could get four blackjacks or four fruit salads or a Barratt's sherbet fountain with a stick of liquorice in it, or Pontefract cakes. Liquorice allsorts. Raspberry drops. Dolly mixture. Gobstoppers. Sherbet lemons. Toffee. All four for a penny — a farthing each.

I'd get sixpence a week pocket money, and I'd go up to the local shop on my trike and I'd get a penny sherbet, some fruit drops, then for

When the advertisement for Rowntree's fruit gums came out, with the little boy shouting 'Don't forget the fruit gums, Mum!' after his departing mother, we were shocked and amazed that any child would be pushy enough to demand sweets every time his mother went shopping.

I had my own ration book, although I don't remember my things being rationed. Daddy's tobacco was, though. We used to go down to Mr Greenfield's and get a tobacco called 'No Name's' which came from under the counter.

tuppence I'd get Barratt's sweet cigarettes, so I could pretend to be smoking on my way home. They were made of sickly white stuff with red ends. Then I'd get a penny Spanish, or liquorice, or a penny pipe. The pipe was a bit of Spanish with a thick bowl on the end with red stuff in it, like those bobbly liquorice allsorts.

I remember how a Mars Bar, which cost fourpence, was a fantastic treat, and we had to share it between the four of us. The knife used to slice through the bar with such precision, in four equal parts. You got about an inch of Mars Bar each.

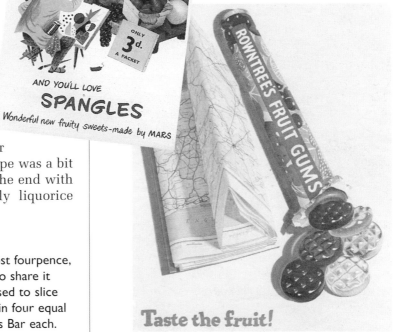

Parents

Parents in the fifties were regarded with a kind of awe by their children. We treated them with respect and we would hardly dare think of answering back. They told us what to do, and we did it. That was simply the way it was, then.

Mothers were godlike creatures in those early years. I don't remember seeing fathers much at all, but mothers were the Voice of Authority. You didn't dare disobey their orders, or talk back to them, or cheek them in any way.

All mothers in those days carried handkerchiefs. And the minute you had the tiniest speck of dirt on your face, out would come your mother's hankie, on would go her spit, and your face would be rubbed vigorously with this horrible scentybreathy-smelling thing. It really was an objectionable habit. Thank God for tissues.

Just about everyone got smacked in the fifties. I can't remember hearing of any parent who was a conscientious objector in that field. A smart clip round the ear for boys and a smack on the bottom for girls was the norm, and no one seemed to think it cruel at all.

If we were doing something we shouldn't as children, my mother would say, 'If you don't stop doing that I'll run away with a black man.'

Adult men in the northeast all spat in those days, although 'Spitting prohibited' notices were beginning to appear in public places. My grandfather once famously spat into the ear of a passing girl, and had to give her half a crown. My father managed to spit into one of my school shoes, kept in the scullery, one day. I only found out, of course, when I put it on.

My father was a railway clerk, and he taught us not to believe in God, not to dance or read novels – 'a complete waste of time', according to him. I don't know what his motivation was, when I think about it now. Maths was okay, though. So I always got 'A's in maths.

My mother was always terribly conscious of, and proud of, the fact that my sisters and I had our own bedrooms. This was really important to her, because she'd had to share a bedroom with several siblings during her own childhood.

Daddy was omnipresent in our family. He used to cycle home for lunch every day from work. He was on a salary, not a wage, which was a very important distinction to our mother.

It was really important to my mother that she was the homemaker. The house we moved into in 1950 was a brand new house, built on a bombsite. It was the most wonderful house Mummy had ever lived in – everything was clean and new. She'd lived in dirty, miserable, horrible old houses all her life, and it was so exciting to her to move into this modern house, with a brand new bathroom. In 1958 we moved into a period house, and I know she was really sad even though it was a lovely old house.

It was terribly important to my parents that we were the archetypal happy family. They would get involved in our school, go to parent-teacher evenings, always come to everything we were in, do the school fete. They were scrupulous about it: you had to keep your children warm and safe and fed and clean and cherished. I think it was because so many families had been destroyed by the war.

My mother didn't go out to work, but every day she would shop, scrub clothes, dust, sweep the floors and cook. It was a full-time job then, keeping a house with children. She didn't sit around nattering to her friends or anything like that.

JON SNOW (B. 1947)
Blue screw-topped bottles of rationed orange juice.
Eggs in waterglass. Talk of war, and fear of it, contrasted with a life in the country of back-lit innocence. Long sunny afternoons, apples in the orchard and tree-houses with walls of hazelnut twigs and bulrushes whose cotton wool heads made us sneeze.

I don't remember Dad any more than most fifties children remember their dads, other than for what he failed to do. I remember him failing to take me places because we never got further than the pub – with me being plonked on the doorstep of the pub with a soft drink and a packet of Smith's crisps, promising not to tell Mummy. One time I wanted to go to the beach very badly, and I had my little ruched spotty bathing suit on under my clothes, which made you feel as though you were wrapped in a carpet roll, and sitting there the whole time and never getting to the beach at all because I couldn't pull him out of the pub. I was so cross with him, and I couldn't tell my mother, so I slammed upstairs which was all I could do.

My father used to stand in front of the range in the kitchen, where we more or less lived because the front room was for best, and say 'God, this is hot' while the rest of us froze because he was standing in front of the only source of heat, blocking it out, while we huddled on those brass fender seats.

My mother went out to work in a munitions factory, and I remember being truly mortified because she wasn't at home to look after me like other mothers. I'd sit in the bus stop, age five, waiting for her to come home every night.

Tradesmen

Home life in the fifties was punctuated by the arrival of endless home deliveries. This was quite normal, and was not reserved for the well-off.

When the milkman, or the rag and bone man, or any number of itinerant salesmen with horses and carts went by, all the women in our street would watch from behind their net curtains. If the horse crapped, they'd all rush out with their shovels and bags. Some almost came to blows, so prized was the fresh steaming stuff, especially for roses.

We'd have all our groceries and greengroceries delivered by Bill in his motorised van. We never bought anything from a supermarket – well, there weren't any, really.

The Kleen-e-ze MAN stands for satisfaction. SEE HIM WHEN HE CALLS! Household & Personal BRUSHES. POLISHES. HAND CREAMS. KLEEN-E-ZE BRUSH CO. LTD. HANHAM BRISTOL.

You only ever see door-to-door brush salesmen depicted in cartoons these days, but they existed, and I felt sorry for them even as a child in the fifties. Such sad specimens, with their boring wares displayed on a tray in front of them, like the ice-cream ladies at the cinema but not nearly so enticing. The best they could hope for was to sell your mother a hairbrush or a toilet brush or a shoe-brush each visit. I wonder if they scraped a living out of it? I suppose they must have.

The rag and bone man came down our street pretty regularly. He was a bit of a con-man, as I recall, and for a big pile of really good used clothes or blankets or whatever, you'd have the choice of a goldfish or a sixpence, but it saved you the bother of trying to get rid of the unwanted goods any other way, and it was exciting, bartering just like in an exotic market or bazaar. He'd come down the middle of the street on his horse and cart, shouting 'Any old rags and bones?' in a singsong voice, the words barely decipherable. It sounded like ennyoleraanbo. It was a sign of the times that you could always hear him, because there just wasn't any traffic noise.

Ginger the milkman delivered milk to our neighbourhood with his horse and cart until the end of the fifties. Sometimes he'd let us travel with him for a while, the cart swaying thrillingly. It was much more exciting than rides at the funfair.

The coalmen were terrifying creatures, bright eyes gleaming out of faces completely blackened by coal dust. They would shoulder hundredweight bags of coal and heave them up the drive and into the coal-shed, bent nearly double under the weight, black dust billowing everywhere. They used to deliver about twenty bags at a time because we lived in a school, and they were notorious for keeping a couple of bags behind. My Dad would watch them like a hawk, and a few times it came to fisticuffs. That was their beer money on the side. It was a tough job, and they probably weren't paid all that well.

The pop man would come every Thursday. He had bottles with those great big contraptions on the top that would take your eye out if you weren't careful. Our favourites were dandelion and burdock, and American cream soda.

A mobile shop would come around the village. And the milk came in a horse and cart, driven by the village idiot. He was harmless enough, and it was a good job for him because the horse knew what to do, which houses to stop at.

The world around us

Cities and towns in the fifties were quieter and more 'rural', and many suburbs looked, and felt, just like the countryside does today. We had a lot of freedom to wander and play. As for current affairs: without television, our worlds were smaller and more circumscribed than those of children today.

Before we had pesticides and main roads and pollution, I remember the amount of wildlife around. Whenever you went out, you'd see things like a shrew running across the path; every pond would have frogs and newts; there were water voles living in streams, insects on the surface. The noise of the birds – it was almost tropical. That gave me an affinity with, an understanding of, nature.

I used to go for a walk every day with my father, after he came home from work, and that's where I learnt about birds, and trees, and wild flowers. There were so many birds in those days. Cuckoos would sing all day. We had twelve species that nested in our garden, including house sparrow, hedge sparrow, starling, spotted flycatcher, greenfinch, chaffinch, blue tit, great tit, blackbird.

I remember the sight of fields of buttercups and daisies, and the smell of fresh-cut grass. Lying in the grass, holding buttercups under each other's chins to see if we liked butter or not. And making daisy chains to wear as necklaces. The ones with fat stems were best, as they were easiest to make a hole in with your fingernail.

Our town had been badly bombed in the war, and the town centre was riddled with vacant lots – bombsites. We just thought of them as our playgrounds. The clifftops had lots of lookouts, too, dug into the ground and lined with sandbags. They were like cubby houses, but unfortunately most of them stank, as vagrants would use them as dosshouses and toilets.

We always used to go to the local farm at haymaking time. The tractors had little seats on the back, and I would sit on the back with this blade inches away. The farmer would pay us village children threepence a row – allegedly – to turn the hay. But nobody ever got paid. We always had cold tea. I suppose nobody had Thermoses then. Half the village would be there. It was terribly dangerous. Haystacks were very unstable, and very big. Once I fell off the top of one and knocked all my teeth out.

I remember the smell of fog, laced with coal dust, in autumn. Burning leaves. The pea soupers in London, which were yellow and phlegmy to look at. The absence of sound.

The first time I stayed in the country, I had no idea that most roads didn't have street lighting, and that it could get so incredibly dark at night. It was very frightening. To see my cousins shoot rabbits and then eat them. To go into the river, which had eels in it. To see foxes. It was so foreign to a city child.

We didn't live in central London, but even so the smog was really exciting when it came. We lived five doors from the corner of the street, and Mummy always used to stand at the front door and wave to us. But on the mornings of the smogs, we'd lose sight of each other way before we got to the corner. The smog was like phlegm in the air. It was yellow, and very bright, and moved, and it smelt very strongly. It also deadened the sound totally. The silence was phenomenal.

I really remember the class system. Our street was a row of workmen's cottages, but we were surrounded by enormous houses with huge grounds and gardeners, and staff and so on. And none of their children were allowed to play with us. They didn't speak to us. The golf club up the road had a class system too, with separate clubrooms for rich members and poor members.

In my first year of high school in 1958, our French teacher asked us what our fathers (not our mothers) did, so that he could tell us the word in French. So everyone said 'My father's a teacher', 'My father's a doctor' and so on. My father was a bricklayer, and – this is the most shameful thing I've ever done – I was too ashamed to admit it. I made something

up. And when I got home that night, I couldn't look him in the eye. It was my first real political lesson, because I remember thinking at the time, 'Hang on, there's something wrong here.' He was my hero, he was the fast bowler in the village cricket team, and yet I was ashamed of what he did for a living.

In those days, a single unarmed policeman could challenge a group of teenagers and they'd all disperse quietly. Now, he'd be taking his life in his hands. But if you saw a policeman then you'd run for your life, whatever you were doing!

My grandfather worked in the local quarry, more or less as they did in the 1800s: we used to go down and wave at him from the side of the quarry, and he'd be wearing trousers and nothing else, just carrying a pickaxe to break the stone. Our village constantly heard the boom of the explosions, and the whistle at one o'clock every day.

My Fifties

SUE TOWNSEND
(B. 1946)
Choking on a gobstopper whilst laughing at a William book. The 'chapped' legs caused by the wet rims of one's Wellingtons. Roaming the countryside, damming streams, lighting fires. Swapping 'jewels' which we kept on a bed of cotton wool in a tobacco tin. Snotty cotton handkerchiefs. Collecting the coal in a coach-built pram. Nightmares about the H-bomb. Newsreel of Belsen. Having nits and worms. Walking three miles to school and three back. Sitting in the yard of a pub with a Vimto and a bag of crisps. White dog shit. Spitting onto mascara. Radio Luxembourg, Sugar Ray Robinson. Deep snow.

What we wore

In the fifties, children's clothes were essentially no more than scaled-down versions of adult clothes. Even tiny babies were dressed in fairly elaborate costumes. There were no romper suits, practical corduroy overalls, cute socks with funny motifs or slippers in the shape of animals. Clothes were fairly sombre and utilitarian, with the exception of nauseatingly frilly, frothy stuff for girls' formal wear. Boys were stuck in short trousers until their voices broke, no matter how bitter the weather, and many had to wear miniature suits, complete with shirts and ties, on formal occasions.

Our mother took my sister and me to a children's fashion parade in a theatre. The posh compere described one dress and the child model lifted her skirt to show 'panties to match'. We thought this was a scream, and to our mother's horror we got up and mimicked the model in the aisle.

Liberty bodices were the bane of my childhood. The rubber buttons were so incredibly difficult for a child's hands to do and undo, especially on a winter's day when your fingers were frozen stiff. And if the day grew warm, you steamed gently inside them like a loaf in an oven.

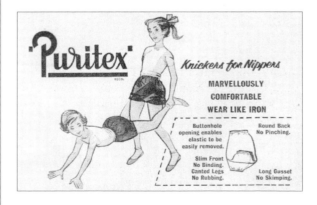

Smart dress was always a kilt, and a handknitted woolly. For parties, smocked dresses with cummerbunds. Being smartly turned out was hugely important to our mothers, and it was very pleasing for us too. I remember feeling terribly sorry for those children with runny noses and turned-down socks and scruffy shoes.

I used to wear huge, bottle green bloomers with a pocket on the front right-hand side. I think it was meant for a purse or a hankie, but I never used it.

My mother was married in 1945 in a borrowed wedding dress, which always made her feel ashamed. But she went away on her honeymoon in a really nice jacket which was described in the local paper as a 'nigger jigger jacket'. I think it was astrakhan. She had it for years. Most people kept their clothes for years and years, then.

My sister and I were dressed in Little Red Riding Hood-type cloaks which we called 'doodie bonnets'. Anything, since, that has a hood or a peak is to me a 'doodie bonnet'.

We always had to have a hankie with us, usually stuffed up a sleeve of our cardigan. They were always white, with embroidered flowers in one corner.

I liked to wear shorts – we wore Ladybird clothes, made out of Viyella. Little sweatshirts with V-shaped necklines, and little grey flannel shorts. I fell out of a tree once and tore them, so I was battling against the girl thing all the time. For occasions when we had to look smart, my mother made my sisters and me matching pleated skirts with little straps. I remember throwing an incredible tantrum because we were being taken to a cricket match and I wanted to wear my shorts, and I was forced to wear the pleated skirt like my sisters. I had to be manhandled into the car.

I remember wearing clothes for a long time, so that sometimes my skirts showed beneath my coat. There was a lot of letting hems down, and letting sleeves down – and you could never get rid of the crease.

I got my first pair of jeans when I was about eight. Before that I'd had a pair of trousers for special, but apart from that I always wore short trousers. Every boy did. We didn't seem to feel the cold at all. We were always out running around.

I got a pair of jeans in 1956, when I was 10. They were very stiff, and not at all comfortable to wear, and they didn't look very nice. But I wanted a pair desperately, and had to bellyache for months until I got them. But for a long time afterwards, women and children didn't wear jeans – they didn't wear trousers.

In the mid-fifties the Brigitte Bardot look came in: tiny waists with wide white belts and huge frilly petticoats (we called it 'full-up net') under gingham skirts. The idea was to get the skirt as near to horizontal as possible. The petticoats always looked fabulous in the shops but once you put a skirt over them they lost all their oomph, and after they were washed they hung limply around your legs like a flag on a still day. I don't think my mother had ever heard of starch.

I remember wearing a cap a lot. Not just at school, but at weekends as well. If a funeral went by you had to take your cap off.

My clothes were always too big for me, because they were hand-me-downs from my older brother. I've got short limbs, so I could never find my hands, and my 'short' trousers were down to my shins. I always looked grotesque, but I never minded because the thought of bothering about clothes or my appearance never entered my head. Getting dressed and undressed was just an interruption to having a good time.

I always wore Clark's sandals, in sensible brown, to school. I used to stare, fascinated, at the shape of the little flower pattern – and I liked to poke my fingers through the little holes and try and pull my socks through them. Apart from that we all just about lived in plimsolls (except we always called them 'daps').

We used to stick these steel things called Blakeys in the toe of our leather shoes. You'd hammer them in, they had cleats. They stopped you wearing out the toes of your shoes, but they made a terrible noise and they wrecked the floors of the school, so in the end they got banned.

I remember Tuf shoes were good when they first came out, they gave a six-month guarantee and had a vulcanised rubber sole.

When winklepickers came in in the late fifties my father wouldn't let me wear them, and I felt terribly isolated when I started secondary school. But I'm very glad now that I never wore them.

Church on Sunday meant wearing my best, and best was awful – it was clothes that just didn't fit me. I had to wear white gloves, with buttons at the wrist, and I hadn't to scuff my shoes, which had been whitened with some kind of stuff by me on Saturday night.

All women seemed to knit in those days, so we always had lots of jumpers. But my Mum wasn't the best knitter in the world, and I was sometimes embarrassed to wear the things she made. The boy down the road's mum was a brilliant knitter, and he had lots of Fair isle jerseys, things like that.

My much older cousin Kathleen wore little feathered half-hats and I thought them the last word in glamour. She and her friends wore dresses and suits with cinched-in waists and flared or tight skirts, hips swaying as they walked. As a beanpole eleven-year-old I longed to have broad hips I could swivel, and a big bum.

Nothing much changed from year to year. When you were ten, you assumed that the clothes you'd wear when you were fifteen would be the same as your fifteen-year-old cousins were wearing – but it fact it didn't work out like that, because just at the point where we turned teenage came the whole sixties explosion, and everything changed forever.

I hated all my clothes, because they were all hand-me-downs. Do you remember that ad, 'Gor-ray skirts, one better'? Well, forty years later I'm still tormented by that ad, because I wore a hand-me-down skirt to school one day and another girl sang this ad to me and I knew that she was really saying, 'That's a bloody awful skirt you're wearing'. So, yes, clothes were important in that they coloured a lot of things that happened to me.

Hair

Apart from the horrors of short back and sides, this section belongs to girls. We went through unimaginable torture to achieve the curls and ringlets favoured in the fifties, whether our hair was long or short.

Hair-washing nights were always a nightmare, because, the bathroom being so cold, you never wanted to expose flesh to it. I had really long hair, and there was no conditioner, so combing it out after washing was agony. I don't remember what type of shampoo we used, or even if we used any at all – was my hair washed in Lifebuoy soap, like the rest of me?

Our mother used to collect rainwater in the rainwater tank outside the scullery to wash our hair in, because it was softer than the lime-producing tap water where we lived. But it didn't help the horror of long hair being combed out afterwards.

ask your hairdresser about
ESTOLAN REG⁰
Conditioning Cream

FOR HAIR
HEALTH &
BEAUTY

now available
for home use
too . . . in

Ogee

2/6 *tubes*

You had to sit in front of the fire until your hair dried, which took forever, then you had to have it brushed out. That caused screams and anxiety enough. But then came the nightmare of getting it done up in rags – long strips of torn-up bedsheets – and I'd have to go to bed like some character in a novel, in my nightie, with these rags tied into my hair so tightly that it gave me a headache. I can still remember the pain. And my hair never retained the curl for long: it looked fabulous in the morning, then it would quickly fall out.

My mother wanted me to look my best for church on Sunday mornings, as most mothers did then, so she would get the curling tongs out and she would think it a good job done when I started yelling as the hot tongs were searing my scalp. The smell of burning hair lives with me to this day. They were very thin, mean-looking tongs and they had obviously done a lot of work as they were completely blackened from having been in the fire, or on top of the Aga where the kettle sat. My mother would wear protective gloves but my head, it seems, was an okay target.

I remember the real aching pain of having my hair scraped back into a bun or a pony tail, or even into plaits. It seemed that if a hairstyle didn't hurt, it wasn't worth doing.

You had to have your hair pulled, it was the norm. Your hair hadn't to have any tats in it. It was yanked every day. And your hair was only shampooed every fortnight, on a Friday. With Drene.

The smell of home perms stays with me from the fifties. My mother and her friends always seemed to be perming each other's hair in the kitchen, and the smell would strip paint. They used these little pink plastic rollers, like tiny bones, with paper wrapped round them. Sometimes our mother used 'setting lotion' on our hair, to force it into waves or curls.

There was such a thing as 'hair sore'. People would say, 'Oh, she's really hair sore.' And what it meant was that your hair was in such tatters that when you brushed it out it looked like rubbish.

Nits were a real problem because we all had such long hair. Suleo shampoo and Derbak combs were our best allies, although the latter crucified you.

You never made a special appointment at the local barber's, you always waited in a queue to have your short back and sides. Dad would always say, 'You're going for a Borstal slash.' So you'd come out with no hair, then a couple of months later you'd do it again. There was no concept of being able to organise your own life.

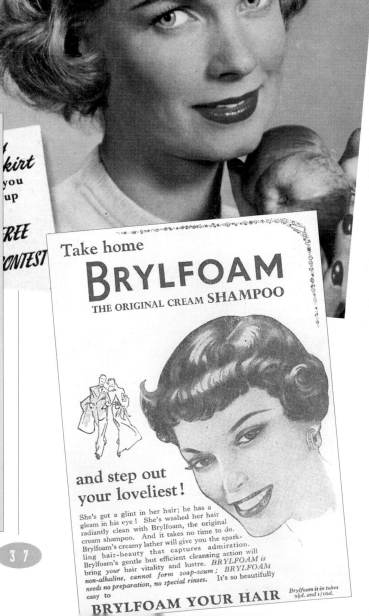

Pets

Pets were an important part of growing up after the war. With growing prosperity, some families could afford to take on extra mouths to feed in the shape of dogs and cats, but then, as now, budgies, goldfish, tadpoles and mice were also highly prized.

We had a budgie who had the curiosity of a cat. He was always nosing around everything, looking for food. One morning my dad came down into the kitchen and found Cheeky Boy in the frying pan, stuck fast. He must have been in the fat, eating the bits of leftover food, when it congealed overnight – which doesn't say a great deal for our cuisine in those days.

My mother used to tell us a silly story about a man with two goldfish called Ella and Emma. But I was terribly upset when my goldfish, Goldie – which I had received in exchange for some old clothes from the rag and bone man – died. My mother just threw the body on the fire before I got home from school. I had been deprived of digging yet another tiny grave in the back garden.

We used to put all the household food scraps into a container called a 'pig bin' in the back garden. The scraps were in fact intended for pigs, and the owner of the local farm would come and empty it once a week – if our dog hadn't beaten him to it.

Our next-door neighbour was a sea captain, and he came back from one trip with a monkey. Everything was all right until one day when it ran up the chimney – we all had coal fires – and of course then it was all over. It ran back down covered in soot and proceeded to scramble over everything. We didn't see it again after that.

I got my tortoise in 1953 and he cost me half a crown. I wanted to call him Jesus, but Mummy couldn't handle that so we called him Charles, after the Queen's son. I'm now on to Charles II.

We'd gather unfortunate creatures from the local pond and keep them in a murky jar for a few days, until they died or Mum told us to throw them away. Anything you could catch became a pet.

We kept tree frogs as pets and you had to feed them on bluebottle maggots. When we went away on holiday we left a load of maggots at the bottom of the cage. We came back after a fortnight, and as we neared our house Mummy cried, 'What's happened to the windows?' They were completely black – every single window in the house was black, covered in flies. All the bluebottles had pupated. For weeks and weeks, as you put clothes on, bluebottles would fall out.

Lots of people kept chickens. But we thought that people who had chickens in the garden were slightly common. Concrete was much classier.

WEEK ENDING OCTOBER 20 1951

EVERY WEDNESDAY

ILLUSTRATED

Juanita, The Gipsy Artist

4d. The Windsor Story—More Intimate Pictures From THE DUKE'S ALBUM

Health care

The National Health initiative meant that post-war children grew up in a more healthy society than any previous generation. We had free school milk, subsidised orange juice, health and dental checks at school. But some childhood diseases were still killers. Poliomyelitis had one final devastating outbreak in 1955 and whooping cough, appendicitis and flu could – and often did – kill their victims.

Chicken pox and whooping cough and other childhood illnesses always had a quarantine period then, and you had to stay in bed for such a long time. You weren't even allowed to take your library books back during the quarantine period.

In sunshine . . .

or in rain! What a picture of glowing health and happiness! What a future of strength and vitality lies ahead for this baby with that right royal Cow & Gate look!

Royal mothers insist on the best that money can buy for their babies. As ten of them have done so to date, why not follow *their* example and bring up *your* baby the royal way, on this Food of kings and King of foods.

Make up your mind to insist on the best, like a Queen in your own right. Get Cow & Gate for your baby too! Buy a tin today!

I had eczema as a child, which got infected and turned into impetigo, so I ended up with huge thick scabs all over my face. And I was terribly lucky, as it turned out, that this happened to me in the fifties and not in the sixties. Because by the time the sixties came along, the treatment consisted of dosing you with steroids. But I had to go to an isolation ward where they treated me by putting a thick mix of starch all over my face every night, covered with a tubular bandage with holes for my eyes. When I woke up in the morning the whole thing had set rigid. Then the nurses would come around with a trolley, with a huge bowl of calamine lotion. They would come into my room and grab hold of the bottom of this cast over my face and pull the whole thing off. With it would come all the scabs. Then they'd cover my face with the calamine lotion. My mother went bananas, convinced I'd be scarred for the rest of my life, but in fact it worked really well and fortunately I wasn't scarred at all.

We had all our injections, but I remember feeling unwell one year while we were on holiday. All sorts of doctors came to see me, but I was okay and went back to school when we got home. My mother told me years and years later that they'd been worried I might have polio. When I returned to school, the girl I'd sat next to the whole of the previous year had had polio over the summer. She was in irons as a consequence. Lots of children wore calipers then.

I used to get tonsillitis a lot as a child; it's amazing that they weren't taken out, but it was a stress-related thing and my doctor thought it was best to leave them in as a kind of built-in safety-valve, which was an incredibly enlightened view for the time. I would get very high fevers, 106° and such, and there was no penicillin at first; I was given this pale pink powdery liquid called Chorylmycetin. It obviously did the trick.

I remember people in our circle having polio in that 1955 polio outbreak. I heard of this thing called 'The Danger List' – I suppose you would call it intensive care now. The word 'polio' then was as frightening a word as 'cancer' is today.

Every time my sister and I became ill as children our family doctor would visit the house. There was no question about it: you were sick, you went to bed, and the doctor visited. Our family doctor was a hearty, jolly man who would invariably shout 'Plenty of jelly and blancmange!' as he left our house. We always groaned. We both hated blancmange, and didn't understand that this was meant to be a treat, not a treatment.

41

The universal cure for a sore throat or a cold in our house was butter, sugar and lemon. Our mother mixed these ingredients up on a plate or a saucer and spooned them into us whether we wanted them or not. The taste was not unpleasant but a bit sickly. It seemed to do the trick, though.

When I was eleven or so I heard a lovely rhyme from a boy in my class. It was a spoof of a then-popular ad for Andrews, the laxative. It went, "Do you wake up in the morning feeling as though the bottom's dropped out of your world? Take Andrews, and you'll feel as though the world's dropped out of your bottom!"

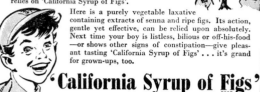
The school inspection was so dreaded. There'd be the nurse, who was always a battleaxe, and the doctor, who was always an old codger, and they'd say 'Drop your trousers and cough' and then they'd grab you. I dreaded it.

I hated the school inspections because you had to strip down to your vest and knickers and the doctor – who was always male – would pull the front of your knickers away from you and peer down them, presumably to see if you had pubes. Quite why they needed to know this escapes me.

Doctors in those days never told you anything. The trend over the years has been this change to open discussion, where they admit they don't know anything anyway. But I remember when you'd go in,

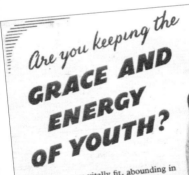

and there'd be this chap who would always be in a suit and a waistcoat, heavy, authoritative, serious, and he'd never really look at you or smile or ask your name or anything. Your parents would say, 'Oh, he's got a pain in his stomach' or whatever, and they'd write a scrip with a squiggle, and that would be that.

It was really important then that you were fit and well. Mummy used to take us to the clinic, where there were posters about what time children should go to bed aged four, five, eight and so on, big posters on the walls showing smiling children.

We were given cod liver oil every day. Even now I gag at the memory. But the example of our dog, who would have killed for it, was held up in front of us. I recently bought some to convince myself that it wasn't so bad. It was even worse than I remembered – but my dogs loved it.

We had orange juice in glass bottles with blue tops. I remember taking the tops off and licking them.

There were red boiled sweetie medicine things, cherry flavoured, and they were disgusting. I still can't eat cherry-flavoured things. They were supposed to soothe sore throats.

I think cod liver oil was free. We'd get a bottle a fortnight. We'd also get orange juice concentrate. They said you needed malt extract

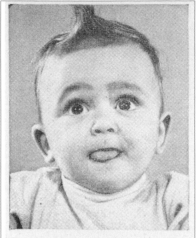

Captain of his side - 1976

He's heading that way – a big, strong boy, straight of limb, brimful of health and energy — thanks to his daily Haliborange.
The vital vitamins, A, C and D, in Haliborange build bone and muscle and help to develop strong, healthy teeth.
Haliborange increases resistance to winter ills and chills. And no youngster can resist the fresh fruit flavour of Haliborange.

Give them
Haliborange
every day

At all chemists
price **3/9**

For teenagers and adults ask for the
NEW HALIBORANGE TABLETS
25 for 3/9, 100 (family size) 11/6
MADE BY ALLEN & HANBURYS LIMITED, LONDON

too, but they didn't supply that. Another 'cure-all' was rosehip syrup. And Scott's Emulsion, dreadful stuff that you took on a spoon. My grandmother swore by Lucozade, which she always brought round for us whenever we were ill. We didn't mind that at all.

It was terribly important to be clean, although we didn't change our clothes every day because there were so few washing machines, and no laundrettes.

Illness in the fifties always meant staying in bed and having the doctor visit you, and having a fire lit in the bedroom. A wonderful aura of calm and quietness, having all day to lie and read or listen to the wireless or colour things in.

Accidents

We had just as many accidents during childhood as previous generations. More, if anything, because we were freer to explore and therefore freer to come to grief.

I always had a bit of an aptitude for maths. I remember thinking hard about probability theory at the age of about seven. So I got this big half brick and threw it up in the air as far as I could, in the back garden, and I didn't look up on the basis that – by the laws of probability – it wouldn't land on me. Needless to say, about ten seconds later I was still standing there when there was this almighty wallop, right on top of my head. I spent three days in hospital. Hundreds of stitches. I've been bald ever since. I can't imagine children now being that naive.

I came off a pushbike and the side of my head was all smashed in. At the hospital they kept taking lots of X-rays, but they'd never do that now because of the danger of radiation. After our experiences in shoe shops, it's a miracle our feet haven't dropped off. Radiation was something that people just didn't understand then.

Children were forever getting their heads split open. I always thought this would be like an egg splitting open, and I was always surprised when I saw these children at school the next day with their heads still on their shoulders.

I have a scar over my left eye where a friend threw a cat at me. I asked him to do it; the cat was in a loft over his garage, and I said throw it down and I'll catch it. And of course it spread its claws out like that, and I did catch it.

Dental care

Dental care in the fifties was comparatively primitive, and fluoride was a distant dream. Most children in Britain had had several fillings by the time they reached double figures, and many had lost teeth. Anaesthesia was effected by administering gas through a face mask, and drills resembled road drills. As a consequence, dread of the dentist was almost universal.

We didn't get anaesthetic when we had fillings, that was only for extractions. And they had those awful low-speed drills. The sound alone was enough to send you into screaming fits in the waiting room.

Dentists in the fifties seemed to specialise in inhabiting dark, gloomy rooms full of clunky dark-brown furniture. They were like torture chambers, especially when suffused – as they usually were – with the smell of anaesthetic.

I remember a smell of rubber, which probably came from the mask they put over your face for the gas. And the horrible dreams you had after the gas. Torture chamber stuff. To this day, I can't bear anyone trying to put anything over my face.

The dentist was hell. 'I can see from my records, young lady, that you haven't been to see me for two years. It says here . . .' Everything was agony.

When I was 11 or so I had several teeth taken out because I had this terrific facial pain and it was just assumed that my teeth were the problem, that it was toothache. When the anaesthetic wore off, the pain was still there. It turned out to be my sinuses, but by the time they found this out it was too late, my teeth had gone.

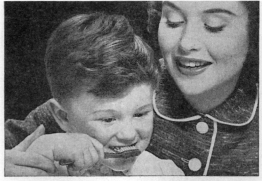

Teach him the twice-daily brushing habit early!

IT'S NEVER TOO SOON to teach your child the importance of regular tooth cleaning. Once his milk teeth are through, it's time to make a start by brushing after breakfast, and again last thing at night. Neglect of these baby teeth will cause pain and may result in misshapen permanent teeth.

A toothpaste that is designed to care for gums, as well as teeth, is obviously best. Any dentist will agree that more teeth are lost through gum neglect than through any other cause.

Gibbs SR contains Sodium Ricinoleate — used by dentists in the treatment of many gum disorders. And, as well as keeping the gums healthy, regular brushing with SR cleans away acid-forming carbohydrates that accumulate on children's teeth and cause decay.

Tingling-fresh

Your child will love the flavour of tingling-fresh SR. And, as well as tasting so nice, Gibbs SR will keep your child's whole mouth healthy and protected.

SR is good for teeth and gums

August, 1957

GR 217-143-100

61

Every child of my age had their tonsils out, and their teeth out. Suddenly, when you were twelve or thirteen, someone – the dentist, I suppose – would say, 'They've all got to come out', and I remember it being a big macho thing: 'I've had ten out' or 'I've had thirteen out'; we'd boast about it.

Hey, Mum! — THE DENTIST SAYS YOU KNOW SOMETHING

The happiest days ...schooldays

INFANT SCHOOL

Children in the 1950s started school at age five. Before then, we had lived at home so school came as rather a shock to the system – despite the fact that infant school was little more than a crèche for the first year or so.

I will always remember my first day at school. I was aged five years and three days, and I was tiny. Next door to me was a boy aged almost six, and he was huge. A monster. All I could think was that I was desperate to wee, and I didn't dare ask how or where to go. We were given a bottle of milk to drink through a straw, and I had to drink it, which made me even more desperate to wee. By the time

I got home that lunchtime – I walked by myself – I was nearly dead. I've spent the rest of my life desperate to go to the toilet. But the really galling part of it was that I thought that once you'd done that stint at school, that was it. I was really shattered to discover that I had to go back that afternoon.

I remember my first day at school, sitting on the desk and crying and crying and crying. Crying all day. Leaving home was the worst hell I could possibly have imagined. Then suddenly, Miss Beverley called us all to sit around her and listen to a story, a Brer Rabbit story. This was a magical turning point in my life. She calmed me down and seemed to understand that I appreciated and understood stories. Within days, I could read and was on my way.

There was no preparation for school whatsoever, before you got there. Mothers weren't allowed inside the lych gate at the entrance. My mother, being a frugal soul from the north, felt that there was no point in buying a uniform to fit a child aged five, as I would so rapidly grow out of it, so she bought an entire uniform for me in size 8 – so I'd get a good three years' worth of wear out of it. As I was always a very small child, the school blazer was tucked back up my arms so much that my arms stuck out almost at right angles to my body. The school hat and shoes were also far too large, and I thought this was a very odd thing, that you had to go to school in clothes that were clearly too big for you. My shoes were like flippers.

My first day at school was untraumatic until two things went wrong: the first was when a teacher came up to us and retrieved me from my mother and said, 'It's okay, pick her up at 3.30, I'm sure she won't cry,' whereupon I burst into tears, thinking, for the first time, 'Maybe my mother isn't coming back'. Then we all sat down at round tables with little round-backed infants chairs, like three-legged milking stools. Then the teacher launched abruptly into the alphabet. She asked who knew how to spell their name. I knew how to spell mine, because it was only four letters, but it wasn't until that moment that I realised that my name was odd. In those days, 'Lisa' was exotic. The whole class was full of Susans, Jeans, Peters, Johns and Gillians, with some Sarahs. Essentially, a sea of Susans. Some children asked me where my name had come from, and I answered, 'My mother'.

I remember a lot of fun, a lot of cutting out and drawing and colouring in and pasting, which was my idea of heaven. Then afternoon sleep time, when we all had to put our heads on our desks round about 2 p.m., and the blinds were drawn, and then came that incredibly delicious drowsiness you felt. It was as though you were in a giant pram, with the gentle snuffling of other children around you and the teacher looking after you. It felt so safe and secure.

Our first teacher reassured us that there was nothing to this reading and writing lark, it was as easy as knitting. Well. I completely panicked, because I couldn't knit. So when I got home that afternoon I insisted my mother teach me how to knit quickly, because this was going to be the key to literacy.

On St David's Day in my Welsh village, we wore full national costume to school. Our mothers stayed up half the night making little black Welsh hats, complete with white lace frills (often made from paper doilies) to frame your face. The hats were made from cardboard which was painted either with black paint or with black shoe polish. They were worn with shawls and pinafores. You had to take your best doll, which could be tricky, as they were often enormous – almost as big as we were – and very awkward to carry about!

Our desks in Infants had holes for inkwells, but of course we weren't allowed to use pens so young, so the holes stayed empty. My aim in life was to be big enough to have ink in my inkwell.

I hated Infants School because it seemed to me to be very strict, and I was frightened of all the teachers. I felt extremely victimised because each classroom had a Wendy house, with cups and saucers inside, and there were certain cloths you used to wipe these cups and saucers, and others you used to clean the floor. One girl went to the teacher and claimed that I'd cleaned the floor with the cloth used to wipe the dishes, and I had to stay in over playtime. And it was all lies. I couldn't believe it had happened to me. It still rankles, hundreds of years later.

To get to our Infants' School, we had to walk through a farmyard. It sounds as though we come from the nineteenth century rather than this one, because there was a duck pond and cart-horses, and hens. The farmer's daughter would come to our house, selling eggs.

PRIMARY SCHOOL

Primary schools in the 1950s were only just emerging from the Victorian influence. We didn't exactly have slates and backboards, but discipline was still very strict. We were expected to sit up straight and keep our mouths shut except when asked a question. We said the Lord's Prayer every morning. We marched in crocodile formation, holding hands. Teachers were gods, just like parents, and children who dared to misbehave were given a smack with the ruler or sent to the head for further punishment.

I remember my primary school teacher frothing at the mouth about boys wearing jeans. (No girl in the early fifties would have dreamed of wearing such things, and only a very few boys did.) The teacher said some parents claimed jeans kept legs clean. 'Nothing,' she thundered, 'can keep legs clean other than soap and water.'

I was very proud of my satchel, which was brown leather with two buckles. My mother had to put extra notches in the straps because I was so small that if she hadn't it would have trailed along the ground behind me.

There was a game played in the schoolyard of my primary school, mostly by boys against girls, but not exclusively. You only got caught once. Another kid would come up to you with an outspread palm, with a bunched fist at the back of it. 'Smell cheese,' they'd say, encouragingly, innocently. You'd thrust your face forward to sniff – and Pow! Your nose would be punched hard by the suddenly propelled fist.

I remember the beanbag as being a very important piece of equipment at my primary school. We used beanbags for all kinds of things, from sport to art, and they always seemed so friendly – just the right size to be clutched in a child-sized hand, just the right weight to be thrown, with a lovely fluid feeling when you squeezed them.

Painting was my favourite. The joy was to do it as neatly and as beautifully as possible, with your tin palette of water colours. Or drawing with Lakeland colour pencils. I could colour in for hours and hours and hours. I thought painting by numbers was great. And you never, ever went outside the lines.

One teacher at our primary school would wait until a pupil was absorbed in something of their own rather than listening to her. Then she'd make elaborate shushing gestures at the rest of the class, tiptoe up to the felon and THUMP the poor kid hard in the back. It's a wonder there weren't any heart attacks, the assaults were so sudden and so violent.

Some of the male teachers we had were far from gentle. Everyone was scared of them. They'd whack kids at the drop of a hat, they'd bang people's heads together, dangerous stuff like that. The sort of behaviour that they'd be taken to court for today. No one complained.

The element of fear was always there. We had the cane, at our primary school. I managed to get it once – well, it wasn't a cane, it was a walking stick. It was a really bad thing to happen, you got your name put in a crimes book and everything. I was only about seven or eight. I pushed a guy over a wall to get a ball and there was an Alsatian dog on the other side which bit him on the bum. Well, he'd kicked my football over the fence and we couldn't play on without it.

I was so advanced as a reader when I went to primary school that I used to have to spend my lunch hours (or dinnertimes, as we called them) teaching those kids who couldn't read. Some of them had nits, and I dreaded getting close to them. I resented this bitterly at the time, and in retrospect I still do.

Nits were such a problem, even with kids who had really short hair. I remember sitting in front of one boy watching a louse make its way up his head. I avoided sitting near him after that, but I got nits anyway. I didn't realise that all the kids in my class had them.

There were huge families of children at our school, really poor children with no shoes and things like that. We'd have a Christmas party, and every child had to take something to eat. I'd take a nice tin with fairy cakes in it; some children used to bring jam sandwiches.

Kids were caned a lot at our school, but I wasn't because I was middle class and obedient. Only the poor kids and the cheeky kids got caned, or at the very least had their hands strapped with a ruler.

Commonwealth Day was a big thing. All the children had to get dressed up as a member of a commonwealth country. All the children at the school were white, so the boy chosen to be a black boy had to have black stuff smeared all over his face. He had a hole in his trousers, where his bottom showed, and we had to put black stuff there as well.

The girls sometimes used to get pulled through the boys' toilets, which was all right except for the smell. Even at eight or nine, there was a terrible smell of blokes. The toilets had no roofs so the toilet paper was kept in the classrooms. If you wanted to go to the toilet during class, you had to put your hand up to ask permission, of course – but you also had to go to the front of the class and specify how many sheets of toilet paper you needed, that is, whether you were going to do big or small jobs. Then you'd run across the playground clutching your paper.

There were 'fever toilets' at my school. There was a row of six toilets, and the first two were known as 'fever toilets' – if you used them, you'd get a fever. We all knew this. So they were never, ever used. It created quite a problem with queuing at the remaining four.

We all played in the air-raid shelters at the back of the school, in the playing field. They were like grassed-over cellars.

BAIRNS-WEAR

school knitwear

Keen on his lessons he may be, but he's full of mischief, too. Never mind! Mother dresses him in the right woollies for work or play— Bairns-Wear school knitwear. She knows they wash like a dream and wear almost forever. Regulation styles and colours for girls and boys of all ages.

I remember so many puddles appearing on the floor at the feet of embarrassed and frightened children. Because you had to ask permission to leave the room to go to the toilet, and sometimes that permission was not granted.

had to sit wherever they could find a space on another kid's desk.

There were 48 kids in my class, and we were divided into four teams of 12. I was in the red team, St George's, and we sat in rows. I was leader, and had a little red badge. We'd have exams twice a term, and you had to stand in front of the class in order of how well you'd done. It was very competitive.

One day we all went out on the school field to play rounders, and everybody seemed to know how to play. Except I didn't. How did the others know? I had no idea what to do. I flung the bat at the ball and ran as hard as I could.

We always had big classes. It was only later that you realised that having 40 kids in a classroom was probably not all that good an idea. Some were just left behind, or neglected. I remember primary school as being really busy – maybe because there were so many kids in each class.

The wall around our school playground was topped with iron railings, but they'd been commissioned for the war effort to make munitions, so in the early fifties they were just stubs. And I thought that was normal, that was what iron railings looked like: inch-high points sticking out of stone.

We had work books to work through, and I was very competitive about getting through them. There were 40-odd of us in our class. We had a mix of whole-class and informal group teaching, and I remember the whole feel was one of teaching excellence. I remember their names and characters, and feel that they're friends still.

I used to get into trouble all the time because I wrote with my left hand, and my writing sloped the wrong way. My hand was slapped with a ruler more than once, for that. I don't know how they got away with it, really.

Our reports were very carefully written, and we always got marks out of 10 for every subject. It was a very structured, orderly way of learning.

We always had a weekly spelling test, and I've never forgotten any of the words I learnt in those tests.

I remember making an elaborate sewing bag cum apron, with a folded-up bit which you put all your bits and pieces in and then you tied it around your waist. It had embroidered patterns all over it.

There were 53 in my class, but only 50 desks. We were seated at the desks in order of accomplishment, but the last three in the class

We seemed to spend an awful lot of time doing really useless things, like embroidering tray cloths or making peg bags or long cylinders to keep spills in.

P.E. classes were held in conjunction with the programme on the radio. There was a huge radio on the stage, and you'd exercise in time with things played on it, such as 'Row, row, row your boat'. We'd all sit there on the floor, energetically pretending to row.

We used to do country dancing in a big way, enter competitions. Morris dancing. There were competitions all over the country, and once a year we'd have a big inter-school country dancing competition at Alexandra Palace.

Our school band had things like clappers, and triangles, and one tinny drum. We weren't encouraged to learn a real musical instrument at all.

Why did we collect jam jars? For a very long time, we were told to collect empty jam jars, wash them and take them to school. We never asked why, of course.

We had to keep scrapbooks on the Royal Family for school projects. I kept one on Lady Mountbatten – now why on earth would I do that?

So much of our news reporting seemed to consist of stories about the Royal Family, especially Prince Charles and Princess Anne. We followed their activities as avidly as any tabloid reader follows the Royal Family's antics today.

The last couple of weeks of the first term of each year were devoted to Christmas preparations. The school Nativity Play, singing carols, making decorations for your classroom, making cards. The festive sense was huge. Before Easter, too, and Lent: Pancake Day, Ash Wednesday. Empire Day.

I remember feeling very confused at school, I felt at a disadvantage because I didn't know what was going on, and why. I had a lot of problems in that respect. People used to talk about getting the scholarship, and I thought they meant you got a ship, in a bottle. I believed that until I was quite old.

When I got into the final year of primary school I knew that the most important thing in the world was to pass the eleven-plus. Then, even when you'd passed, the next most important thing was choosing the right school and getting into it. I can remember taking the envelope up to my parents, who were in bed. And I'd passed.

We used to be called 'grammar snobs' by the kids who hadn't passed the eleven-plus. In a way, it was more of a stigma to have passed than not, in my Welsh village.

I remember doing the eleven-plus for three Saturday mornings running, in the local high school. We had an English test one Saturday, a maths test the next week, then an IQ test. I'd never done an IQ test before, so I guessed most of it, not realising that this could have affected the rest of my life.

BOB AYLING (B. 1946)
I remember growing up in the leafy Surrey suburbs: short trousers; girls with plaits; Montessori school equipment; copperplate handwriting; the shadow of war stories from my parents; lots of bicycling (which was safe then); working in my father's grocery shop in the holidays and learning to count change in pounds, shillings and pence, which improved my mental arithmetic.

Sunday School

These are the recollections of Church of England children, because that was the prevailing religion of the fifties. We were possibly the last generation to attend church regularly.

My sister and I went to Sunday school for years, mainly to collect the pictures they gave you for good attendance. Then for some reason we rebelled and decided we'd play truant, playing in the fields near us during the time we were supposed to be in church. But we couldn't bring ourselves to spend the collection money our mother gave us, so we'd throw the lot into the field behind our house when we were sure no one was looking. There must have been a fortune scattered around there in the end.

I got a cup for never missing a day of Sunday school for a year. I used to go with my father to this chapel on Sunday afternoon, they'd have a musical do, a mixture of prayer and music. I can remember them playing 'Lilac Time', then a fire and brimstone preacher would bang on. Very odd.

You'd get a picture, a stamp, every week for attending, and you could stick them in an album. That was the best thing about going. The pictures were of Christ on the Cross, or somebody going into a burning bush. If you filled the album, you got a Sunday School prize. You did your best to get as many stamps as possible.

My father grew up in a strongly Methodist working class family, and my mother came from a more liberal Church of England family. So I ended up having to go to church three

times on Sundays. But I have really happy memories of it. I was involved in plays and performance and acting there. The first time I ever appeared on stage, I must have been about three, was singing 'Over the Rainbow' at Sunday School. Going to church was what you did. You had to put your best clothes on and sit there in this draughty ancient Gothic building.

We weren't allowed to play out in the front garden or the back garden on Sundays. You could go outside, but you weren't allowed to make a noise. And we weren't even chapel people.

I didn't get christened until quite late. I remember the day I was christened, in white clothes almost like Confirmation clothes, and I had the little white gloves, the little white dress, the little white shoes and the little white socks. I desperately wanted a pair of frilly socks, but my mother thought they were common so that was that. I asked her why I was being christened, because I knew my name, and surely everybody else knew it, including God. But of course I had to go through with it, and I was too small to reach the font and too large to be held in someone's arms, so they put me on a hassock and the priest made the sign of the cross on me, plus two circles. I said in a very loud voice, 'Why has he written Oxo on my forehead?'

I remember the rituals: Christmas, Easter, harvest festivals. Immensely cosy rituals, with wonderful hymns. There was a big harvest supper every year in the village in the Memorial Hall. That was a major celebration.

The harvest festival at our church was a bit embarrassing, really, because I think the original idea was to take some of your own produce in to be distributed to the poor and needy, to give thanks for the bountiful harvest on your own land. And of course we all lived in a town and had tiny gardens and were lucky if our parents grew a couple of tomatoes in a greenhouse. So we ended up taking bought stuff, some of it in tins, in the end, and it all got a bit silly. There were always loaves of bread at the front of the display. I reckon the vicar got most of it.

'Walking Day' was a procession of witness for the church: you witnessed that you were a believer, and you carried banners with streamers. You had to wear a posh frock to carry a banner, which proclaimed things like 'God is Love'. All the girls on any one banner had to have dresses made of the same material, so we'd go into town together and get flocked nylon, which you only ever wore on Walking Day. You wouldn't dream of ever wearing it again. But the good thing was that you could go up to people on Walking Day and smile nicely and introduce yourself, and they'd be obliged to give you threepence. Threepence!

CHRIS WOODHEAD
(HM CHIEF INSPECTOR OF SCHOOLS B. 1946)   My Fifties

I remember standing at the end of our road spotting car numbers – no more than a couple of cars every ten minutes – now, of course, a constant stream.

I also remember the horse-drawn milk floats, the trolley buses and the fog, and men in bowler hats.

The coach ride to Weston-super-Mare for summer holidays took forever on the A4. If I wasn't sick before the coffee stop at Maidenhead, I knew I'd be alright.

As for school, I recall the rows of desks, the fairly competitive classroom ethos, the horror and incompetence I felt when confronted by compulsory needlework.

PART 2
Fun and games galore

What we played with

It's true that we had far fewer toys than children do these days. If you got a handful of presents each birthday and Christmas, you were doing well. So we did have to rely more on our imagination, on found objects, and on fantasy and make-believe.

Toys

The rigid divide between girls' toys and boys' toys was alive and well in the fifties. But, so soon after the war, we were lucky to have toys and a safe environment to play with them in.

JUNE 1956

VOL. XLI NO. 6

MECCANO
MAGAZINE

My sister and I had lots of peg dolls. It seems so sad and austere now, to have dolls made out of wooden clothes pegs, but they were just as interesting and enjoyable to us as more elaborate dolls.

My mother once made me a doll out of some lengths of black wool tied together at the top. She was no more than a pompom with a sewn-on face, really, but I called her Dot and loved her dearly.

Now, there's everything to assist imagination. But in those days we had to be imaginative ourselves. Things like Meccano sets – they're plastic now, but any lad who had a Meccano set in the fifties knew about tensions; knew how tight to do something up; had that feel already. Men and their Morris 1000s!

All the boys in our neighbourhood had train sets. I'd beg and plead to play with them, and had wonderful afternoons when permission was grudgingly granted. But as a girl I had no chance of ever getting one of my own. This was understood implicitly – it never even occurred to me to ask for one. But then, it wasn't the trains that interested me, it was the villages and towns and countryside the train sets travelled through.

We all had these French knitting machines, which were nothing more than a hollow wooden tube, a bit like a cotton reel, with four or five wire hoops bent into the top. You twisted the wool around each one in turn. What came out the other end was an endless thin sausage of knitted wool, and the really hard part was figuring out what on earth to do with it.

I still have my autograph book from 1955. I'm the proud owner of the signatures of Steve (The Bachelors), Mike Preston, Bruce Welch, Hank Marvin, Wee Willie Harris and Jimmy Young (twice).

I was given dolls, but because I had a brother and male cousins they never lasted long. Especially the one with the china head. I loved that doll, but it didn't last a minute. The only durable doll I had, the only one to survive my male siblings, was a rag doll.

My biggest thrill was on my third birthday, receiving my pedal car. I was so delighted; it was that moment, that joy, that sticks in my mind more than anything from my childhood.

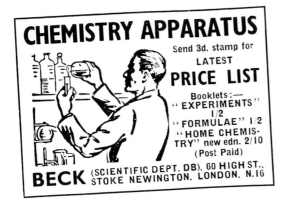

Children could buy the most amazing chemicals over the counter then. I used to get iodine from the chemist's and ammonia from the hardware shop and mix them together. This resulted in an unstable ball that was in effect a home-made bomb, which would go off unexpectedly (a touch from a feather duster would be enough to set it off) and at length – pop, pop, pop, pop. I can't remember the chemical formula because of course all my chemistry books were destroyed in one final attempt to control the substance. I also used to buy hydrochloric acid.

I still have my Triang pile-driver, and people can't stop playing with it. It's wooden, and you push the bits of wood in and they whoosh out. It's fifty years old now, but I don't think it was new even when I was given it. Lots of toys then were hand-me-downs.

My brother and I used to play shops with the old ration books, once they weren't needed any more.

My father made a lot of my toys. I had a wonderful train made out of paint tins that you could sit on. He also made me a farm out of corrugated paper and mirrors.

Dad got me a balsa-wood kit to make a glider. You could buy a tiny little jet motor, called a Jet-X, I think, to put in it – a little cylinder with a sort of combustible tablet to put inside. You put a wick in one side, screwed the end in, and it gave a sort of jet propulsion for a couple of minutes.

I had a tricycle that I rode to my grandparents' house – I had to cross the main Bristol road. Then they moved, and I had to ride it over a mile to their new place. No one thought it dangerous, or odd. It was assumed that everyone would look out for children.

Look what he's built with *BAYKO!*

And with the numerous parts contained in each set there are many models of all types of buildings that can be constructed to either your own design or to the plans we provide.

PRICES
(including Purchase Tax)

No. 0	Standard Set	14/-
No. 1	Standard Set	21/-
No. 2	Standard Set	31/6
No. 3	Standard Set	52/3
No. 4	Standard Set	99/3
No. 0X	Converting Set	7/-
No. 1X	Converting Set	10/6
No. 2X	Converting Set	21/-
No. 3X	Converting Set	47/-

BAYKO

OBTAINABLE FROM LEADING STORES AND TOY SPECIALISTS

Manufactured by PLIMPTON ENGINEERING CO. LTD., LIVERPOOL 1

that used to secure fencing wire to posts. Hit me right in the eye. He also fired a fire extinguisher in my face once, because it looked like a gun. I was blinded for about half an hour, and had to have drops in my eyes for weeks afterwards.

My father had a childless brother, Uncle Dick, who made me my dolls' house. I can still remember the little latch at the side. He wallpapered it for me, and painted it, and made every single piece of furniture in it. It was modelled on a Nottingham terrace house. He made toys for me in his shed: little boxes to put things in.

Everybody seemed to have a little farm, with miniature animals. They were really popular. I used to save all my pocket money to buy plastic cows – called Bluebell and Daisy – and horses (the carthorse was always called Dobbin) and ducks. I don't ever remember buying a sheep, or a goat.

In the years after the war, guns were all the rage. Guns and crossbows; weapons in general. My friend made a crossbow once and nearly took my eye out. It was a crossbow that fired those staple nails

DINKY TOYS

No. 716
Westland-Sikorsky Helicopter
Length overall 3½ in. 2/6

No. 735
Gloster Javelin Delta Wing Fighter
Wing Span 3½ in. 2/6

No. 131
Cadillac Eldorado Tourer
Length 4¼ in. 4/6

No. 106
Austin Atlantic Convertible
Length 3¾ in. 3/3

No. 455
Trojan 15-cwt. Van
'BROOKE BOND TEA'
Length 3¾ in. 2/9

No. 443
Tanker 'NATIONAL BENZOLE'
Length 4⅛ in. 2/11

No. 670
Armoured Car
Length 2⅝ in. 3/3

No. 621
3-ton Army Wagon
Length 4¼ in. 5/3

No. 164
Vauxhall Cresta Saloon
Length 3⅞ in. 3/-

No. 190
Caravan
Length 4½ in. (including towbar) 3/11

MADE IN ENGLAND BY MECCANO LTD., BINNS ROAD, LIVERPOOL 13

Just like the real thing!

Airfix kits are not just models — they're exact replicas, each series to a constant scale.

Airfix 1/72nd scale Lancaster bomber. 17" wing span. 7/6d.

Aircraft (*all* to the same 1/72nd scale), 00 gauge railway accessories, vintage cars, historical ships. Airfix value is *unbeatable!*

Nearly 100 kits from 2/- to 7/6d.

AIRFIX

THE WORLD'S GREATEST VALUE IN CONSTRUCTION KITS
From Model and Hobby Shops, Toy Shops and F. W. Woolworth

[A159C]

VINTAGE CARS
1930 Bentley 2/-

HISTORICAL SHIPS
H.M.S. Victory 2/-

STOP PRESS !

Latest Airfix Production

YEOMAN OF THE GUARD

Beautiful 1/12 scale model Beefeater. **2/-**

Also new—SEA HAWK jet naval fighter-bomber. 1/72nd scale. British or German markings. **2/-**

We had lots of jigsaws. The Cinderella Pantomime Jigsaw was always done at Christmas, then it was covered by the tablecloth to keep it from being scattered. We had several featuring armadas and sailing ships – to this day, I look up at certain cloud formations tinged with pink and shout, 'It's a jigsaw sky!' Sea and sky.

The main board game was Monopoly. Nearly everyone seemed to have that. And Ludo, and Snakes and Ladders.

I got a pedal car, which was very unusual for a girl. It was maroon, with a white steering wheel. Living on the side of a hill, there were very few places I could drive it. There was a crazy paving path leading from the back of the house to the shed, so I drove my car down the stairs and along this path, then out into the road like Toad of Toad Hall. I lost control halfway down the hill and cannoned into the local policeman. He took me home, I was smacked and the car was impounded. I still loved it, though.

We didn't have lots of toys compared with children now. But my wish-list always had board games on it — I especially liked the classics like Chinese Chequers, Tiddly Winks and Ludo — and I would spend literally hours playing with them. I suppose my parents thought it was a good way to keep me quiet. But I've never forgotten how pretty they were, the sound of the dice in the cups and the slippery feel of the counters. The colours and patterns have always stayed in my memory.

Neighbourhood games and sports

With little traffic to interrupt us, most of us played out on the streets of our neighbourhood if there wasn't a local park. We have a shared memory of childhood spent predominantly outdoors, despite the notorious British weather.

No street was without its hopscotch lines chalked on the pavement. It was mostly a girls' game, like skipping; I don't remember any of the boys ever playing.

Scraps were a huge craze. We'd spend hours, days even, swapping scraps. We bought the scraps, then we swapped them. The favourites were very Victorian – women in crinolines, girls with violets, cherubs, baskets of flowers. To look at them now, they seem to belong to the nineteenth century, not the 1950s. But we loved them. They're still around, of course, but adults use them now for decoupage.

LESLEY O'MARA
(B. 1954)

I remember the highlight of my preschool days was Andy Pandy. Of course, there were no mother and toddler singalong or baby gyms in those days! The little boy from next door used to come in and watch it and I remember thinking how babyish he was because he used to cry when the theme music started to indicate that it was over for the day.

Bill and Ben was nearly as good. I particularly liked WEEED but I bought a video of it a few years ago when my children were small and they thought I was mad – couldn't see the point of it all! Shame the children have changed so much.

We played a lot of juggling games with balls, or 'stotting' them against a wall. I remember one rhyme for two balls went:
Shirley Eaton, Shirley Eaton
She's a star – S-T-A-R!
Other rhymes were:
'Mademoiselle from Armentieres
Parlez-vous?'
and
'House to let
Apply within . . .'
and
'I'm a little Dutch girl
Dressed in blue . . .'
and
'Jelly on a plate, jelly on a plate
Wibbly wobbly wibbly wobbly
Jelly on a plate.'

The older girls, the fourteen-year-olds, were brilliant at skipping. We used to use the washing line in the street, and it was enormous. Two strong lads would hold the line, one at each end, and we'd all chant *Salt, Vinegar, Mustard . . . PEPPER!* and the boys would swing this huge rope, starting slowly on salt and going as fast as they could on pepper. Only the older girls could handle that. We'd play along the side of the road. If a car came someone would shout 'Car!', but it didn't happen often enough to seriously disturb the game.

A whole lot of us would play 'What time is it, Mr Wolf?' out on the street. You had to creep up on 'Mr Wolf' by taking the number of steps he called out as the time – three o'clock would mean three steps, and so on – but the idea was to cheat and tag him before he could tag you.

I seemed to spend half my life standing on my head against a wall, or doing handstands.

Cowboys and Indians were really popular – although I didn't know anyone who had an Indian outfit, we were all cowboys. The whole of the local village would play; the game would go on for days. Every so often you had to die, and lie there on the ground. Then you'd get fed up with that, and join in again. We all had guns, but you'd always run out of caps and have to go 'Pow, pow!' It was a fabulous game, although there was no rhyme or reason to it, none at all.

Every winter the whole gang would sledge down a steep neighbourhood street on a variety of home-made and bought sledges. It's a wonder there weren't more accidents, but about the worst that happened was some of us – me included – going home crying with the cold after an hour or so. I'd have to practically thrust my hands into the fire to thaw them out after making snowballs.

One thing we did in a big way was make trolleys, soap-boxes, particularly if you lived in a hilly area. It was all to do with the design of prams. They had two big wheels and an axle, and you could take the wheels off and sign an IOU to your friend for 2s/6d to get his axle. Then you could make your own soap box with wood, and put a brake on, and a steering wheel. I remember one I made, an eight-wheeler, which had two-axle steering, and four of us could sit on it and shoot down a hill. Another was like an armoured car: a box, essentially, on top of a trolley, and you'd go along steering it and have a little slit to look out of, and all the other children would throw all these bricks at you, so it'd be bang bang bang down the hill. You couldn't possibly do that today because it's so dangerous.

Life was just a total game, we played games non-stop. Things like eating or sleeping or going shopping or having your hair cut were just interruptions to having a good time, playing cricket or football.

LORD (MAURICE) SAATCHI (B. 1946)

I have no memories of childhood. Life on earth began at the age of 11, getting off the 210 bus at the stop outside our new house in Highgate, after my first day at my new school. Apart from knowing the street where I lived in Hampstead, what happened for the preceding 11 years is a blank. Psychiatrists would have a field day...

There were four other boys my age in our street, so we had a proper gang. We spent most of our time outdoors, playing football, cricket, anything involving a ball. We never played with girls.

There was a wood just up the road, where we had our favourite tree – the old oak tree. If I couldn't find any of my friends, or they weren't home, I'd just go up to the old oak tree and there'd be someone there. We climbed it, swung from it, built platforms and houses in it. It was like our headquarters. As we grew older we reached higher and higher branches.

We played this game called Kick the Can. It was like Hide and Seek, except it featured a can you had to get back to unseen, and kick it to win.

I used to pinch golf balls from the local course and sell them at a shop in town. I stole Cliff Michelmore's golf ball once. He was a terrible golfer and his balls always landed in the rough. It was my prize possession for ages.

We didn't have any swimming lessons at school. You left primary school at 11 or 12 unable to even swim. We taught ourselves to swim at the local pool – you just learned by hammering away at the water for a while in the deep end. If you didn't swim you would drown, so that's how you learned.

Hobbies

Hobbies were part of post-war childhood. You were expected to have a hobby, by your school, your parents and even by your friends. It was part and parcel of the 'Devil makes work for idle hands' philosophy that ruled how children's time was spent.

Everyone in the world had to have a hobby in those days. I could never understand the attraction of stamp collecting, but we did it, simply because everybody did. If I had to fill in a CV form today, I'd probably put 'Stamp collecting' under 'Hobbies or Interests'.

We used to spend our pocket money on little packets of stamps from the Post Office. You could get a large packet of mixed stamps, which were mostly rubbish, or small packets of more select stamps.

We (and by we I mean boys) all used to collect birds' eggs. It was part of climbing trees and falling off.
The impact on nature was not that great, I hope. We only ever took one egg from each nest. I used to stick pins in moths and butterflies, too. But they all rot, eventually.

We used to go to tap dancing classes in a big hall over the Co-op. We'd dance to 'Papa Picolino'. I had little red tap shoes.

We were each given our own small patch of the garden to cultivate and tend. I remember the joy of growing love-in-a-mist, marigolds and forget-me-nots. I still try to grow those flowers, and other old-fashioned species from our garden then, such as hollyhocks, foxgloves and wallflowers.

The whole family played cards every Sunday afternoon. Knockout Whist, a form of rummy, and Newmarket with matches. Occasionally the adults would bet with money and let us kids win. A halfpenny each, or something.

I used to collect train and bus numbers, and I'd save up my pocket money to buy the books that had the numbers in them that you crossed out when you spotted them. An anorak from way back.

We belonged to the 'I Spy' books. You could join the club, and you got sent badges and things.

Social life

Social life in the fifties, especially for children, was a rare creature, seldom seen. But what we did have was a very strong sense of family, and an equally strong sense of community, of neighbourhood.

The highlight of my social life when I was about eight or nine was visiting my friend's house for tea. She lived a few houses up the road, but it was very exciting to go there and have banana sandwiches, and sometimes her mother would get us those cut-out cardboard dolls with paper clothes and little flaps to keep them on. Bliss!

Our parents belonged to various clubs – the Round Table and the Ladies' Circle were the main ones – and they seemed to be forever going out to glamorous events such as Fancy Dress Balls, which involved endless preparations and costumes and our cousins coming to babysit. Our mother would always be very excited on the day, and when she finally appeared in the living room wearing her ball gown, or costume, or whatever, with her hair done in sausage rolls and wafting trails of Chanel No 5 or Evening in Paris, it was as though we'd been visited by an apparition from Hollywood or New York. They once went to see a local production of *Call me Madam*, and for months afterwards they'd burst into 'There's No Business Like Show Business', dancing around the kitchen flourishing imaginary top hats and canes.

We used to love going to the neighbourhood Beetle Drives. 'Beetle' was a dice game where you had to draw the outline of a beetle on a sheet of paper by filling in the details – body, head, feelers, legs, eyes – according to the numbers you threw with the dice. The first on each table to complete the beetle won that round, then all the round winners would compete for the grand final. Beetle Drives were so exciting.

I remember learning to dance and going to neighbourhood dances in scout halls, austere places with chairs lined around the walls. We danced the Valeta, and the Dashing White Sergeant, and the Gay Gordons. They were good fun.

No one ever came to our house except relatives, and we never went out except to visit relatives. The only house I ever ate at, apart from our own, was my grandfather's. I ate there every Friday, before Cubs. I'd have bacon and egg.

Eating out was virtually unheard of in fifties suburbia. Once in a blue moon our mother would take us to a local department store cafeteria for tea; she and her friends would sit sipping tea and watching the mannequins – as they were then called – modelling the latest fashions.

I have a strong memory of the fact that in the mid-fifties, families would go for walks together in the evenings. These were pre-television days, so there were no distractions, and the big

social occasion of the day for us was the evening walk. The number of people outside in the evenings was phenomenal, and the world had a far friendlier feel. I remember just walking around, seeing so many people, talking at corners and so on. Cars and TV were the start of the social isolation of many neighbourhoods.

My parents had some friends we used to visit occasionally, and I can remember thinking them so exotic, so strange, because they were a married couple but they had no children. They were the only such people I ever met as a child.

What we joined

Joining things – societies, charity organisations, quasi-military set-ups – was also part and parcel of growing up in the fifties. Few of us escaped the net entirely.

I was a member of the Boys Brigade, which had a more military bearing than the Boy Scouts. It was the forerunner of the Cadet Corps, for boys round the age of seven to eleven. We went on camps, marched around, and did things like first aid, working with wood. It was fun. We went on one huge expedition to Exeter, which was an early insight into how friction can occur because the guy in charge fell out with the officer and stormed off in a huff. I still have my hats and badges.

My mother was a Brown Owl, so I joined and got all my badges. I remember polishing those bloody badges! She was really strict about it. By the time of the Guides, I'd lost interest. I remember the Jamborees at Wolverhampton. We all sang, and had to dance up this middle aisle towards Princess Margaret. And there were loads of competitions, including Greek dancing, which everyone did then, very expressively.

I joined the Brownies but I was sacked because I stole the subs money to spend on sweeties. I couldn't see the point of Brownies anyway, all that dib dib dib stuff. I could never learn to tie the tie, so I'd pull it over my head – but Brown Owl would check to see if it was freshly tied each week. This was another tyranny I could do without. I think I was an elf, or a fairy, or a sprite. I did quite like the fancy dress element, though: Brownie parties, where I went as a carrot.

We belonged to Enid Blyton's Busy Bees, which meant that you raised money for the PDSA, essentially. We read about each other's exploits in *The Enid Blyton Magazine* – subtitled 'The Only Magazine I Write', which made Pa laugh. On page 2, there was always a letter from Enid Blyton, from 'Green Hedges, Beaconsfield, Bucks', telling us about her children.

GIRL ADVENTURERS

This was a club that readers of *Girl* could join, provided they filled in one of the coupons in the magazine and sent it in with a postal order for one shilling and sixpence. In return they would receive a club badge – a delightful brooch of a girl's head in gilt, with the words 'Girl Adventurers' underneath it – and a membership card which listed the club rules:

'Rules

1. GIRL ADVENTURERS will:

a) Enjoy life in a way that helps others to enjoy life too. They will not enjoy themselves at the expense of others.

b) Strive to develop themselves in body, mind and spirit. They will feel it is their duty to make the best of themselves.

c) Work for the good of all around them.

d) Be thoughtful for the needs and feelings of other people.

e) Set an example of kindness to animals.

f) Give up part of their own time every day in order to help others.

2. The GIRL ADVENTURERS exist:

a) To promote the ideals of living outlined in the rules.

b) For comradeship between all who accept the rules given above.

c) To organise meetings and expeditions for members.'

Club activities included Hobbies Advice Bureau, Pen Pals Group and Holidays:

'During 1955 in cooperation with the Youth Hostel Association we were able to organise our Walking and Cycling tours. These proved to be even more successful than the 1954 series. One of the greatest concessions for club members is our *GIRL* Ballet Scholarship scheme run in association with the Royal Academy of Dancing and the Sadler's Wells School, and many Adventurers took advantage of it last year. They also took part in the *EAGLE/GIRL* National Junior Table Tennis Tournament Competitions, Carol services, Circus visits and Christmas Parties. If you are not already a club member – join now!'

Party time celebrations

THE CORONATION

It was the biggest party of them all, a national celebration when whole communities got together to cheer the ascension to the throne of Queen Elizabeth II in 1953. It was also the first complete memory of past events many of us have.

Oh God, the coronation was such an exciting concept. That gold coach with all the horses, and the queen with her crown and ermine-edged robe, and the orb and sceptre – just like every fairy tale coming true. But the actual event was a bit boring. We crammed into a neighbour's house along with about a million other people to watch television for the first time. We took sandwiches and a Thermos flask. It went on and on and on, and there really wasn't much to hold the interest of a six-year-old. The two tortoises in the garden were much more interesting.

LOYAL GREETINGS

from the brewers of

DOUBLE DIAMOND

A DOUBLE DIAMOND WORKS WUNDERS

SOUVEN

Week Ending J

ILLU

UE **6**d 953

THE CORONATION IN WONDERFUL PICTURES

TRATED

With commentaries by
Sir Compton Mackenzie
H. V. Morton
Lord Kilbracken

The whole neighbourhood went to a party in a huge Nissen hut in the middle of the prefab estate. All the girls over a certain age were given a locket with a picture of the Queen and Prince Philip inside, but I wasn't old enough so all I got was a Coronation mug. My sister was given a locket, and I was so upset and made such a fuss that three lots of neighbours brought lockets to me over the next couple of days. I felt so ashamed, and had to hide the fact that I already had a locket from each of the last two.

"IN THE NEWS"
Scrap Book

for Press cuttings, Photographs etc,

I remember going into Swansea to watch the Coronation, and getting a little model of the coach and the double line of horses, and the gilt coming off the coach very shortly afterwards.

The people opposite us painted the boulders in their front garden with red, white and blue stripes, and put bunting out, so I knew it was going to be a really important event.

In school we had little kits and we made the coach and horses up out of pre-pressed cardboard, pop them up and glue them down. At the neighbourhood party, I got a Coronation mug, took it outside and dropped it.

My Dad bought me a sparkly cut-out model of the coach and horses and we assembled it into a 3-D model. It was the perfect size to fit in the fanlight of our front door. One house up the road had a model of the lion and the unicorn in the garden, it was there for years, a local landmark.

My Fifties

GENISTA McINTOSH
(B. 1946)
February 1952. I remember standing with my father in thick fog on Westminster Bridge, queueing to file past the coffin of King George VI as he lay in state. We don't have fogs like that any more.

FESTIVAL OF BRITAIN

The Labour government decreed that we should all start to enjoy ourselves and shake off the post-war gloom. A great festival exhibition celebrating the achievements of the country and Empire was built on an old bomb site on the south bank of the Thames, opposite Charing Cross. By the time it opened in 1951 the government had lost a snap election and was replaced by the Conservatives. The incoming party was less than enthusiastic about the festival, but the public flocked to it in their thousands. Britain loved the whole enterprise, from the 'Skylon' – that pointed upward like a futuristic rocket – to the 'Dome of Discovery'. It was extraordinarily ambitious but visually stunning.

I remember going to the Festival of Britain in 1951, and going on the Tree Walk. It was this really exciting elevated walkway through the trees in Battersea Park. Because I was so excited, I can see it now if I close my eyes.

My aunt and uncle took me to see the Skylon and as we walked across Hungerford Bridge I caught glimpses of it, along with the Dome through the iron work. It seemed to take forever to cross the footbridge that ran alongside the rail tracks and I thought surely no one can walk this far. The only exhibit I can remember is a man making cricket balls. I *was* only six.

I couldn't really work out what the Festival of Britain was for. An uncle who was rather better off than us actually went to London to see it – and he brought back the souvenir brochure. I remember staring at the pictures, trying to figure out what it all meant – what was the Skylon supposed to do? We did have a huge street party though – all the kids wore their best clothes and sat at lines of tables which our parents had carried out into the street. They served amazing treats like pink blancmange in decorative moulds, ice cream; tinned fruit and Carnation milk – and we all tucked in for Britain.

During the Festival of Britain the whole village went into a frenzy of decorating the streets red white and blue. My father copied the festival symbol – a sort of shield with the head of Britannia on it – and stuck it proudly in the centre of the front railings. Britannia was flanked by red and white paper ribbons. As for my mother, she made hundreds of paper roses in red white and blue and attached them all over a large branch of a tree which she stuck in the front garden. It looked as if the tree had suddenly grown all these red white and blue roses. As for the rest of the village, it was the same story: houses absolutely groaning with red white and blue bunting.

The grown-ups celebrated the Festival of Britain in the most exciting ways. I remember they arranged a football match between the men and the women in the village. We were totally shocked to see our mothers dressed up in football kit – showing their pudgy little knees. But they loved it. They broke all the rules, kicked the ball wherever they wanted and threw the ref into the river when he tried to blow his whistle to call them offside. We children were laughing ourselves silly in the stands and cheering like mad!

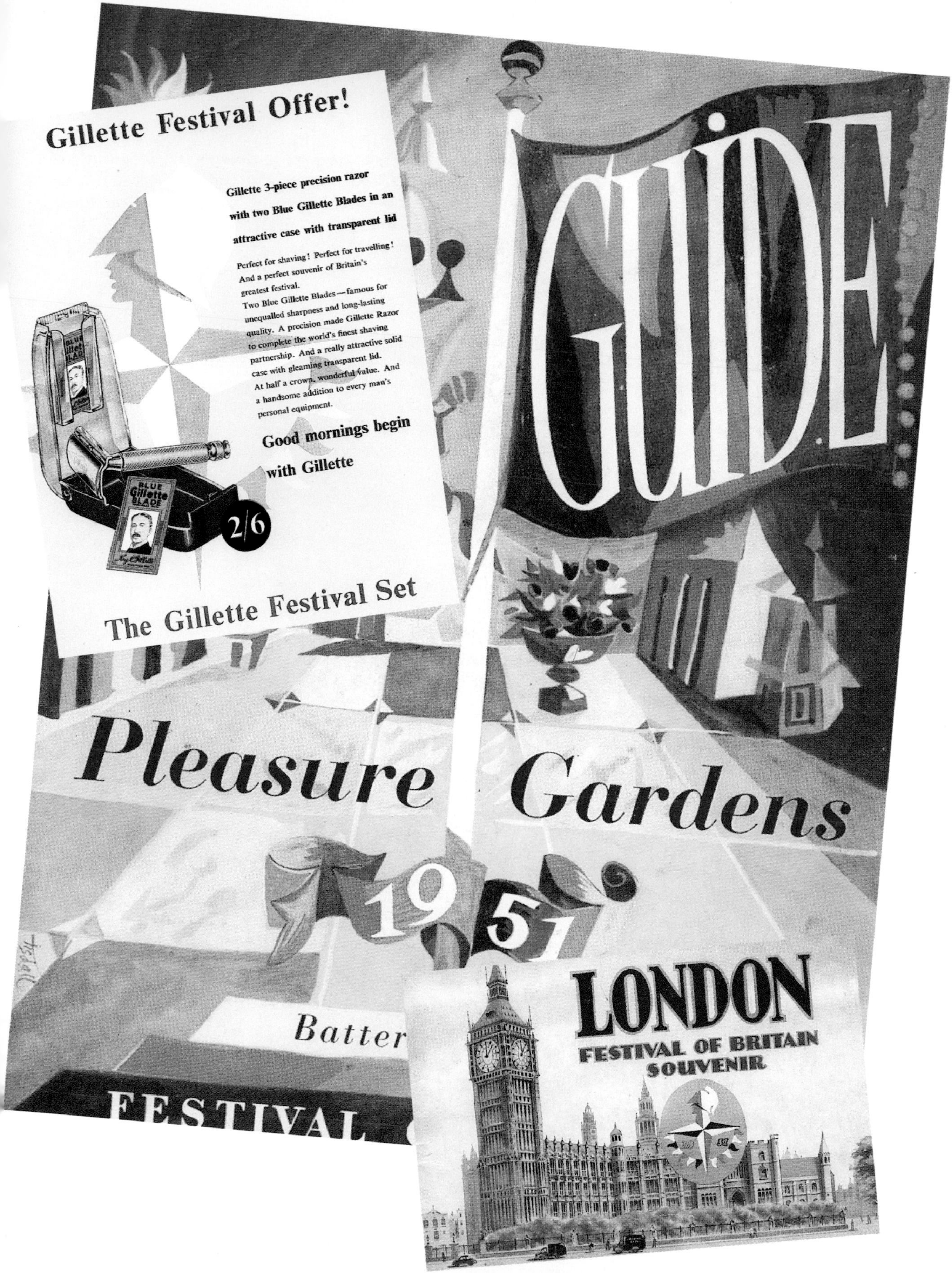
Gillette Festival Offer!
Gillette 3-piece precision razor with two Blue Gillette Blades in an attractive case with transparent lid
Perfect for shaving! Perfect for travelling! And a perfect souvenir of Britain's greatest festival.
Two Blue Gillette Blades—famous for unequalled sharpness and long-lasting quality. A precision made Gillette Razor to complete the world's finest shaving partnership. And a really attractive solid case with gleaming transparent lid. At half a crown, wonderful value. And a handsome addition to every man's personal equipment.
Good mornings begin with Gillette
2/6
BLUE Gillette BLADE
The Gillette Festival Set
GUIDE
Pleasure Gardens
1951
Batter
FESTIVAL
LONDON
FESTIVAL OF BRITAIN
SOUVENIR

BEL MOONEY (B. 1946) — My Fifties

It is about 1954 and I am in my Nan's house in Liverpool, rummaging in the drawer in her fifties kitchen unit. It smells of food; there are paper bags spotted with grease, carefully smoothed and folded; bits of string and elastic bands wait for usefulness. I take out the stained ration books, and examine them curiously, before continuing the search for glue. She and I are going to make cushion covers from squares of saved black-out material. She cranks her hand-operated Singer energetically and creates the covers. Then it is my job to draw big petal and leaf shapes in coloured felt, cut them out, and stick them on. Once the old pads are stuffed in she shows me how to sew up the open sides – and there are the new cushions. I am as proud of them as of the new powder blue suit with velvet collar and pleated skirt my mother has made me. So busy we were – frugal and clever.

BIRTHDAYS

Fifties birthday parties closely resembled those of today, except that no one had such things as paid entertainers or jumping castles. But traditional food and games held sway: fairy bread, jelly, lemonade, 'Pass the Parcel', 'Musical Chairs', 'Blind Man's Buff', 'Pin the Tail on the Donkey'.

For my sixth birthday my mother organised for several of us to go to the Grotto, a local restaurant built into a cave at the bottom of a cliff – the height of sophistication. That was exciting enough, but the real treat was that she hired a taxi to take us there and back. It was the first time I'd ever been in a taxi, and the last for several years after that.

At one party I won a beautiful shiny bangle for reciting 'I know a man named Michael Finnegan, He had whiskers on his chinnegan . . .' and I was so proud of it I insisted on wearing it to bed that night. When I woke up in the morning my bed was full of bits of bangle.

We always had a birthday tea, with lots of jellies and pop, and bridge rolls, cut in half with fish paste or boiled eggs inside. And iced gems. We had proper party frocks, with rosebuds on them and sashes at the back.

I always had a big party in early October, I remember the weather as always being pretty good. I'd get some great presents, annuals like *Rupert Bear*. We had fizzy drinks and fairy cakes, the usual, with kids making themselves sick. But I never invited any girls.

Today you're 7
QUEEN OF SCOTS
60120

All our birthday parties were identical, and they all had the same people at them, but on your birthday you were the special person, which made all the difference. Blowing out the candles was the most important ritual: blowing them out in one go made you a real man. None of these universal candles you get nowadays that come alight again after you've blown them out.

GUY FAWKES NIGHT
The smell of cordite in the sharp autumnal air remains a powerful memory for many of us. In the days before strict legislation, danger ruled okay.

One of the women in our street was a great organiser of street parties, and every year she'd buy a whole lot of fireworks for Bonfire Night. All the neighbourhood kids would gather firewood and we'd have a big bonfire in the vacant lot. One year, she'd spent a lot of money on fireworks for the whole gang as usual but one of us dropped a match into the box and they all went off together.

Kids could buy fireworks easily in those days – you could steal them pretty easily, too – big bangers and rockets. Once we opened up some fireworks and took this huge amount of gunpowder out to a tip, then put it into a big metal container to make a bomb. It didn't go off, so my pal went over to have a look. Just as he looked at it there was an almighty flash – I think he was lucky to survive, let alone be able to see.

Dad used to ceremoniously nail a Catherine Wheel to the old shed, just like about a million other fathers all over the country, and like them he'd watch it fizzle out half the time. I think that was part of the fun, the tradition of Bonfire Night: all these dads running around trying to be important, failing to make a good firework display.

EASTER
Very much the poor cousin of Christmas, Easter was nevertheless celebrated with eggs, and cards, and, in many towns, parades.

There'd be an Easter Parade through the town every year, and you'd march along with your palm cross, and every year the weather would be foul. Women and children would struggle bravely along in their wispy finery, clutching their Easter bonnets against the howling gale and shivering in the icy rain. It became part of our family language: 'clutching your Easter bonnet' meant doing something outdoors in typical English weather.

We always got something new to wear for the Easter Parade. If you didn't, the crows would crap on you and you'd have bad luck. It was a well-known fact. So I usually got a new coat.

Our grandmothers would send us eggs every year, through the post, so of course they arrived in pieces. A lot of the chocolate had this fatty, vile taste, too, especially the cheap stuff from chain stores. It really had to be Cadbury's.

On Easter Sunday we'd have dyed boiled eggs. Ordinary eggs boiled in water with a bit of food colouring or dye in it.

ROYAL VISITS

The imminent arrival of a royal visitor sent town councils into overdrive in the fifties. New paintwork, special cleaning – even new loos.

Princess Margaret came, and they built a special toilet for her. The whole town was up in arms. Especially because as soon as she went it was taken away.

The Queen's visit to our town was a major, major event. All the schools sent their pupils to line the streets at designated places, and we all had little Union Jacks to wave. It was very exciting, even though all we saw was a car and an arm in a window, waving. The cavalcade itself was pretty impressive.

We were all given a flag to wave during the Queen's visit, and told to put it on a stick. I forgot to ask my parents in time, and at the last minute my mother gave me a knitting needle. So I had to hold the flag on the knitting-needle stick and wave it as best I could.

" *How happy could I b* *with either !* "

. . . and how happy we shall be when this famous Shortbread can be offered in the full quality of its ... excellence.

CHRISTMAS

Christmas held a very special magic in the fifties, and although that sounds like the worst, most schmaltzy cliché ever, it also happens to be true. Christmas in the fifties was the last bastion of naiveté. We believed in Santa Claus coming down the chimney clutching a sack full of presents; we believed in happy families under the mistletoe or gathered around the Christmas tree, in Rudolph and Prancer and Dancer and the rest of the reindeer. We even believed in the little Lord Jesus, asleep in the hay; in the shepherds watching their flocks (or, more cynically, washing their socks) by night; in the three kings following yonder star. The traditions and beliefs of a Christian festival were very much more to the fore, and the crass commercialism we now know was only just beginning to raise its head. Because television wasn't widespread until late in the decade there were no 'Christmas specials' to look forward to; instead, we acted out nativity scenes at school, went carol-singing around the neighbourhood, played charades, made execrable Christmas cards and nativity scenes with cardboard, cotton wool and cellophane paper, and spent the weeks before the day itself in a frenzy of excitement. It really was the biggest event of the year.

Man - about - the - house slippers in tan leather with warm felt linings. 19/11

Put your feet up cheerful slipper fleecy wool top sponge soles in most colo

Embroidered moccasin bedroom slippers in a variety of colours — just the thing for chilly mornings. 23/11

The kiddies just love these jolly slippers with Prudence Kitten on the toes. From 9/11

Let Christmas comfort be your gift this year. There's a wonderful range of practical presents at prices you can afford at your local branch of

True-Form

Christmas began every year with carol-singing, about a week before Christmas. That's when we made all our money to buy Christmas presents.

I wish I could relive the excitement of those freezing Christmas mornings, waking in the pre-dawn and tingling with excitement at the day to come. Not just the presents and the food, although of course they were wonderful, but the camaraderie. The socialising – to neighbours' houses for a glass of sherry for grown-ups and cordial or green ginger wine for us; then getting in the car and driving through the snowy, slushy streets to relatives, to exchange presents and drink and eat more. Hearing all the beautiful choirs singing carols, and singing along yourself. And everyone being so jolly and so friendly. It really was the most enjoyable day of the year – better than your birthday, even.

I'd spend the two weeks leading up to Christmas combing the house for presents. I still don't know where Mum used to hide them.

Each year we'd buy a dozen day-old chicks, then on Christmas Eve my father and I would go out the back and slaughter them all for Christmas. That was our Christmas present to our relatives: a chicken. We'd wring their necks then hang them upside down and slit their throats so that they bled to death. Then we'd pluck them.

We had real candles on our Christmas tree, with real flames, clipped onto the ends of branches. Why didn't the house burn down? The decorations were lovely: little glass goldfish, so beautiful.

I always associate cigar smoke with Christmas, because my father had a cigar only on one day of the year, and that was Christmas day. Same with celery: Christmas day was the only day we ever had celery, and the smell of it still reminds me of Christmas.

Christmas was so exciting. So wonderful. I believed in Father Christmas until I was about nine, until someone told me. Like all children then I truly believed that I heard him creeping into the house on Christmas Eve. I didn't get expensive presents, I only ever got one thing plus a stocking. And the stocking always had a mandarin covered in tin foil in the toe; Brazil nuts, which no child actually likes; hazel nuts; some Cadbury's chocolates; little tin stocking fillers; and always a book. And then you'd get the annuals which didn't fit in stockings, such as *Film Fun*, *Radio Fun* and later *Girl's Own* and *Girl's Crystal*.

There were hundreds of us in my family who'd get together at Christmas at my grandparents' house, and we'd all play games such as 'Pass the Ring'. You'd all sit around in a circle, with a piece of string going around everyone, and there was a ring strung on it. You'd all sing, something like 'One Man Went to Mow, Went to Mow a Meadow', and you'd pass this ring along the string from one to another, and the person stood in the middle had to guess who had the ring when you stopped singing. My father said I once accused my grandmother of having it on her finger, and she nearly lost her false teeth laughing.

"Old Favourites," says Mum

— how well I remember, when I was but little older than Molly is today, the perfect joy of reading my "Strand" and munching my

Mackintosh's

— But Molly has no time for reminiscences. She's all for the present pleasure—especially when it's

Mackintosh's

She thinks their toffees and chocolates are simply wizard, and lets it go at that.

JOHN MACKINTOSH & SONS LTD. HALIFAX

My parents didn't have much money but there was always plenty of bits and pieces, enough to fill a pillowcase left at the end of the bed. And Dad used to make things for us – little wooden boats, aeroplanes.

I'd get maybe a skirt and jumper on the end of my bed, but nothing was ever wrapped in paper. And there were no bits and pieces either, no stockings. But I didn't feel deprived at all.

My brother and I had twin beds in this perishing cold bedroom, and our presents were put in a pillowcase on the end of the beds. We always tried desperately to stay awake, but never managed. We'd wake up at half past five and discover this full pillowcase each, and we were allowed to open one thing. Then, shivering with the cold, we took our pillowcases into our parents' bed and we could delve into them and open the rest of the presents.

At eight o'clock on Christmas morning half the street would be out booting around these brand new footballs and things – ruining them, of course, because they weren't meant to be used on tarmac.

Like everybody else we had chicken for Christmas dinner. No one could afford turkey, it just wasn't an option then.

Christmas dinner was like nineteen Sunday lunches rolled into one. There had to be the turkey, the bread and butter sauce, the sprouts, the pudding with the sixpence and the holly on the top. Plus mistletoe, paper chains, fairy lights, Chinese lanterns, Advent calendars. I never made a wish list, because I hoped in an osmotic way that Santa/God would know what I wanted deep down, without being told. Santa just brought you things. But the great thing about Christmas was eating. The big boxes and tins of Cadbury's Roses, Quality Street, that you didn't have much of during the rest of the year. And the nuts, and the oranges.

Boxing Day was our party, and the whole neighbourhood would come over to our place. We'd play games like 'Murder in the Dark' – it was so frightening if you were going to be murdered – and a game where you had to say what you did first thing in the morning. My auntie used to go out the door and, when people answered things like 'I look at the clock', she'd answer, 'Don't you do this?' and pour a jug of water into a bowl, which of course sounded like someone weeing. And everyone cried laughing, because in the fifties this was the height of naughtiness, of daring.

Blackpool Rock and Brighton Pier

HOLIDAYS

Not every family could afford to take holidays: money was tight after the war, rationing was still in place – at least at the beginning of the decade – and not many people had private transport. But many did manage. The idea of the family holiday really took off in the 1950s. And if the holiday wasn't in an exotic resort, and if it consisted of a week in a caravan or boarding house at a dour seaside town or a series of day trips in the rain, it was nevertheless magic for us children. Golden memories of childhood holidays don't need sun, or foreign climes or cuisines; they just need that glorious sense of freedom, of not-school, not-home, of difference – different streets, different smells, different names – to add up to juvenile paradise.

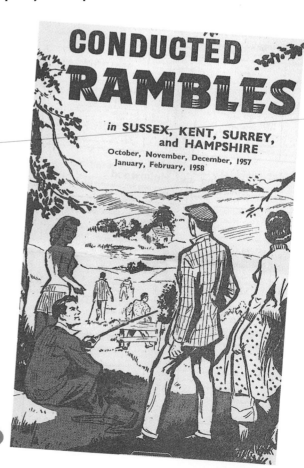

WHERE YOU WILL MEET THE KIND OF PEOPLE YOU'D LIKE TO MEET

On your Butlin holiday you are sure to enjoy yourself among the finest array of entertainments, amusements and amenities obtainable anywhere — and all included in the All-in Tariff. In your sleeping chalet at the edge of the sea and in your dining hall you are surrounded with service. At Butlin's you do no more for yourself than you would expect to do at any first-class hotel. Come to Butlin's this year and enjoy a *real* holiday.

FREE BROCHURE: *Send postcard to*
BUTLIN'S LTD. (Dept. H.B.), 439 OXFORD STREET, LONDON, W.I

We had summer holidays in cottages in places like Clacton. We took all our stuff there, and the carrier would come and collect all the luggage in advance, in a big tin box. It took seven days for your stuff to get to Munsley or Clacton or wherever. So, for seven days, your best clothes would be in the box, which made them all the more desirable. To this day, I call my favourite clothes my 'luggage in advance' clothes.

We'd have an annual holiday in the caravan site in Llandudno, and Father used to borrow a car for it. People used to do that in those days – lend a car to a friend so they could take their family away on holiday. It seems extraordinary now. It was a very small car, and the four of us would barely fit in. But it was really lovely, I have great memories of these holidays.

We often spent our annual holiday in Devon, which was a 13 or 14 hour drive from where we lived in Yorkshire, with Dad clutching the steering wheel and trying to keep the car going straight, because suspensions in those days weren't quite what they are today. We used to stay in what were called 'apartments', where you had your own bedroom and sitting room, and you bought your own food, but the landlady cooked it for you. There was still rationing then, which I think was the main reason for this arrangement, because the landlady couldn't go out and buy food for everyone.

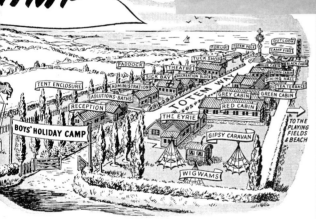

Grand Competition Story!   **£100 worth of Prizes!**

REX MARKS THE SPOT!

by GEOFFREY MORGAN

WHEN Dick Fenton turned the bend in the leafy lane and saw the open white gate and the gaily painted buildings of the Boys' Holiday Camp at Gileston he knew that the picture in the camp brochure had at last come to life.

The camp lay in the beautiful Vale of Glamorgan. The sea was on its doorstep and the wooded slopes of the Welsh countryside rose gently behind it—a delightful setting for holiday adventures.

In company with new friends, and escorted by a Camp Courier, who had met them at Birmingham, Dick entered the camp and headed for Reception.

"This is it!" he thought. A fortnight of fun was about to begin.

The camp atmosphere took him back to Redskin encampments. To his right, on a smooth lawn, stood a cluster of wigwams and a gay gipsy caravan. Beyond were "The Eyrie" and the sleeping-cabins—red, grey, green, brown, blue and black, and again beyond these was the camp fire site and a tall lookout tower.

A rose-bordered roadway ran between the cabins and groups of other one-storey buildings on the left. This road was known as Totem Way.

Mum and Dad had a tandem with a sidecar, when I was very small. They went all over the east coast on it with me in the sidecar; there wasn't much traffic. I remember going to Dungeness and riding on the miniature railway they had there – I think it still exists. But apparently when I started standing up and jumping around in the traffic I put a stop to all that.

We couldn't afford to go on a family holiday every year, but regardless of that I used to go on a two-week camp to Bognor Regis with an organisation called the Highgate Camp, which never cost more than £5 all-in. It was organised along old military lines, boys only. It served a purpose, getting some boys away on a break who otherwise wouldn't get away in the school holidays. We had tent inspections, but there was plenty of sport, swimming at the beach. We always had good weather, hot; we'd come back brown. The water always seemed warm.

Royal Blue
Inclusive Holidays
1957

DEAN & DAWSON LTD.
IN CONJUNCTION WITH ROYAL BLUE SERVICES

Southend was a kind of workers' paradise for Londoners, for East Enders, in the fifties. The Kursaal is German for a room where you can have fun, but the Kurzal, as it was called, was considered irredeemably common. Southend Pier, the longest pier in England, was a mile long, with a little railway that ran along its length which used to give me complete nightmares because I was convinced it would one day fall into the sea with me on it. The whole town was full of jellied eels, and cockles and whelks, and candy floss and Southend rock, and fortune tellers and donkey rides, and Punch and Judy shows.

When we got to Filey or Scarborough or wherever, the local children would all be waiting outside the railway station with bogies – trolleys to take luggage off to the boarding houses and digs. Very enterprising.

To be stuck on an English pier must have been truly suicidal for the performers. But to a child, even Punch and Judy people looked so glamorous. The seaside itself was magical. You never seemed to want for entertainment, or food, or deckchairs. The deckchair man would come along with his little ticket roll, and you'd be able to sit in your deckchair for your allotted time.

OUTINGS

Family outings ranged from local walks to day trips into the countryside or to the coast. The spread of the motor car meant the inevitable rise of the 'Sunday driver'.

Focus on
BRIGHTON AND HOVE

My parents never did get a car, so we went everywhere by bus. We went to lots of museums. The Commonwealth Institute opened while I was at school, which was a big thing for us. We never bought food while we were out, we always took sandwiches. Occasionally we were allowed to buy a drink, but I always chewed the paper straw to shreds, which drove my father insane, so we didn't get them very often.

We went on lots of outings to Blackpool, Morecambe and Southport, by train because we didn't have a car. Lots of fun to be had: donkey rides, sandcastles, ice creams, candy floss, fun fairs. It was always wonderful, amazing. We loved it.

Not all northern towns had holidays at the same time, because it wouldn't do to have all of Bury, Bolton, Wigan and Preston to go to Blackpool together. So Wigan had holidays at the same time as places like Glasgow. It was a very volatile arrangement – there were horrendous fights, drunken evenings. I've never had so much tremendous fun as when I sat on the boarding house steps in Blackpool singing with the drunks from Glasgow.

We always had a car: a Ford Prefect, then a Vauxhall Viva, a Vauxhall Wyverne. They were biggish, bulbous cars with leather seats, lots of chrome and wooden dashboards. We used to go out to Breedon on the Hill, to watch the cricket. There was a canteen and paddling pool and a picnic area. I have lots of

SUNDAY EXCURSIONS

FROM

PADDINGTON

AND

EALING BROADWAY

DURING

DECEMBER, 1957

Paddington Station, W.2.
October, 1957.

K. W. C. GRAND,
General Manager.

WESTERN　BRITISH RAILWAYS　REGION

JENNI MURRAY (B.1950)
When I began researching my history of women since 1945 I came across a *Woman's Weekly* of 1954 (I was four then) which came with the paper every Tuesday. In it was a pattern —THE pattern — for the knitted swimsuit my mother made for me. Suddenly I was back on the beach at Scarborough. Grandpa in his shirt, tie, socks and sandals. Grandma with crimped white hair, flowery frock, and a little too much foundation. Mum in a crisp shirtwaister, daddy handsome and slender in immaculate white flannels — all in stripy deckchairs in a chill wind. And little me leaping over the icy waves of the North Sea as the woollen cossie became weightier and weightier and finally slipped down to expose — oh horror — my chest!

photos of The Picnic – the cloth spread on the grass, and my mother in her sundress with a gathered top and a big flowery skirt, posing with the basket and all its special picnic cutlery, and Thermos flasks, and chicken legs, and egg and cress sandwiches with the crusts all cut off. We children were left to amuse ourselves, more or less.

Outings in those days weren't as frequent or as expected as now. Parents didn't feel obliged to keep children moving in the same way; parents then didn't see it as their life's obligation to keep us entertained. The idea was to keep us socialised and obedient.

We'd go to the Epsom Derby every year. That was a big day out. There was an amazing character there called Prince Monolulu, a bookmaker. We were allowed to have a bet on the Derby, and one year I won. The horse was called Hard Ridden, I think, and he was about 20-1. I had threepence each way on him – it was a Big Bet. When you only got a penny a week pocket money, threepence each way was a Big Bet. So I won a lot of money, and I've been a gambler ever since.

GETTING AROUND
We were far more reliant on public transport in the fifties. Sometimes it was wonderful, but at other times it left an awful lot to be desired.

We'd go to school on the trolley bus. Trolley buses were excellent because you could listen to the post, and the sound would tell you how close it was. But every other trip the antennae, or whatever they were called – those big feelers that stuck out the top of the bus and attached to the lines – would come off at a particular corner, and it would take ages for the conductor to get them back on again. And sometimes they would crackle just like lightning.

The bus conductor would have a long row of different tickets in little containers slung around his neck, and he'd pull one out and punch it before handing it to you. If you went upstairs on the bus you'd be practically asphyxiated, because everybody smoked up there. But it was worth it because it was much more exciting upstairs.

I spent my first train ride, apparently, banging on the doors and screaming to be let out. I think mainly because the train was so disgustingly smelly with cigarette smoke and unwashed bodies. Public transport then was really rather gross. You'd finish up a train ride with your mouth and nostrils choked up with coal dust and smoke, and buses, especially the double-deckers, were indescribable.

'Hello, children, everywhere'
The media and us

BOOKS AND LITERATURE

In pre-television days books and comics were all the more important. Once we were over the book-torturing toddler stage books became prized objects, the only medium other than radio and infrequent films able to transport us away from the mundane into wonderful imaginary worlds. Enid Blyton seems to have been our favourite author by a huge margin.

I loved the stories in *Girl's Crystal*, 'The Three Marys', and the stories of being in girls' schools. The endless stories of the orphan who was brought up by the wicked and cruel

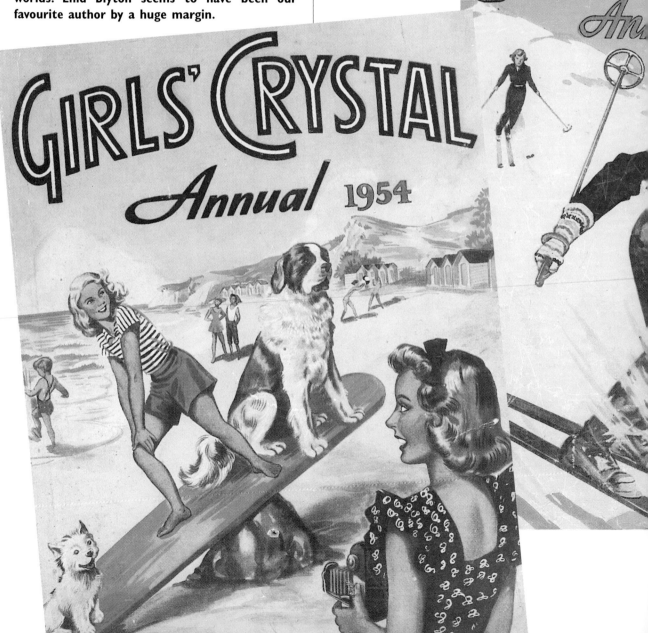

and dismissive family, who turned out to be the rich person's daughter or the princess; we all wanted to be that. The joy of getting the annual, and sneaking back upstairs to read it.

Annuals were really important. We used to get the *Girl* annuals, and the *Swift* annuals. But we were definitely told that Enid Blyton wasn't quite what was approved of. So I'd always try to borrow her books from friends and read them illicitly.

I read all the G. A. Henty books, which were called 'Books for Boys', despite the fact that I was a girl. Books like *With Clive in India*. There was a boys' shelf in the library, and I got right into those books.

One of Noel Streatfield's books featured a heroine who could fly a plane and became a pilot, and that was such a role model for me. Mostly, books featured girls who lived in enormous houses or went away to boarding school, whose fathers were away in India or wherever, and I couldn't relate to them at all. I never read a book about a school where people lived in ordinary families, in ordinary homes.

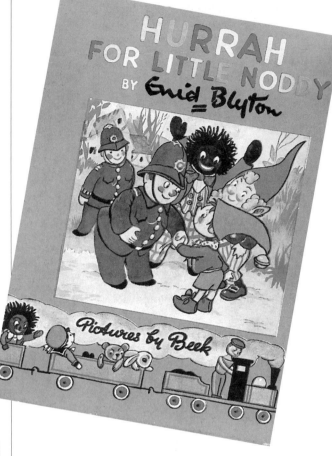

All girls in books were uniformly silly and soppy, apart from George in the *Famous Five* books and William Brown's friend Joan in the *Just William* books.

Whenever a new Noddy book came out, my father would buy it and bring it home for me. I particularly remember number seven, *Noddy by the Seaside*, because I'd been waiting for it for so long. It was pale blue.

I was desperate to have the same sorts of adventures the children in Enid Blyton books had. I loved the *Famous Five* books, but best of all were the *Adventure* series: *The*

Mountain of Adventure, The Sea of Adventure, The Island of Adventure, and so on. I still think they were every bit as exciting as *Raiders of the Lost Ark.* Anyway, I wanted to have those adventures, so for years I diligently made sure that my pockets were full of such useful items as string, compass, pocket knife, notebook, pencil, etc, in readiness for being kidnapped, or coming across escaped criminals, or a bank robbery in progress, or whatever. Needless to say . . .

My play world was based entirely upon the adventure model. I didn't read any of the classics such as *The Wind in the Willows* or *Swallows and Amazons.* I read stuff on my parents' bookshelves – stuff they told me not to read, such as *The Tribe That Lost its Head* by Nicholas Montserrat, and *The Seven Pillars of Wisdom* by T.E. Lawrence, and *The Singer Not the Song* by Audrey Erskine Winthrop, set in South America, which I read three times, I was completely enthralled by it.

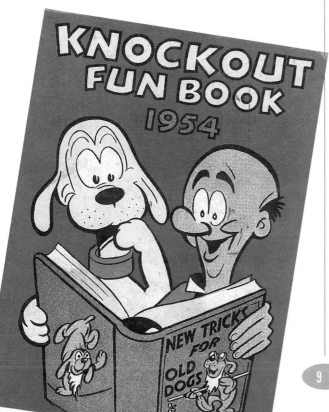

I read all the time as a child. Most books came from the library – my brother and I would go to confession at St Coleman's church on Saturday morning with my dad – then on to the library – new souls, new books each week! My own most precious books were *Little Women, What Katy Did, What Katy Did at School* and *What Katy Did Next.* Also, of course, I had *Little Men, Good Wives* and *Jo's Boys.*

My cousin used to send me her old annuals – I didn't care a bit that they were last year's books. The excitement of opening that parcel and seeing the covers!

COMICS
Comics provided enormous fun and enjoyment, but were often frowned upon and even banned by well-meaning parents who had no idea what the term would encompass in subsequent years.

Tuesday night was comic night. My sister and I would spend the early evening at our Nana's, and the excitement began when the comics were delivered at about 5 o'clock. The glorious sound of those magazines hitting the floor as they came through the letterbox! We'd get *Chick's Own,* then *Dandy* and *Beano,* later *Girl* and *Bunty.* They were all such a joy.

I used to read *Sunny Stories* when I was very small, then I had *Girl.* My brother had *Eagle.* You could hear them being delivered, because there was no other background sound.

We were given something called *The Children's Newspaper* which was extremely tedious. Terrible. We wanted *Dandy* and *Beano,* but we weren't allowed to have them.

I had to fight to get the *Beezer*. Before that, I was allowed to get *Girl*. I looked down on *Bunty* because my parents did.

I got loads of comics, because my mother worked in the local newsagent's. They were all last week's, but who cared. There was *Lion*, and *Eagle*, and *Rover* and *Adventure*, and then *Rover Adventure* because they'd merged. I read them all avidly, cover to cover, except for the obligatory 'educational' feature in the middle, about butterflies or whatever. The Bash Street Kids were my favourite. Lord Snooty. Keyhole Kate.

POSY SIMMONDS
(B. 1945)

From our home in rural Cookham we would go to London for our holidays. London was so filthy then, when you got back you had black bogeys. And smuts. And you always gave your newspaper to the engine driver of the train. It seemed to be expected.

The most exciting thing was getting to know American children at the air base nearby. Americans seemed so glamorous: they gave us Hershey bars and Coca-Cola and American comics with Superman and Sad Sack and Caspar the Ghost. At home we had *Dandy, Beano, Robin, Swift, Eagle* and *Girl.* I preferred *Wendy* to *Jinx*; Wendy's hair was black with a blue sheen on it. I thought *Belle of the Ballet* a bit wet. I called her Belly.

Most of all I adored Willans and Searle's *Molesworth* books, *How to be Topp,* etc. We all went around saying 'Chiz chiz' and calling people Fotherington-Thomas (the utterly weedy wet).

The best thing about the end of the 1950s was getting to join Yardley's Teenage Club, which sent you samples of bright pink lipstick. Pink Magic was my colour: I slapped it on.

What we listened to

Sounds were all important in the days before television. The radio was a wonderful source of stories and music

RADIO

'It's quarter to two, Mummy! Quarter to two!' This was the catchcry of our early childhood, as we made sure that our mother had the radio tuned to our programme and the armchairs and cushions plumped ready for that magical time, 'Listen With Mother'. For half an hour, we'd be lost in the stories, songs and poems featuring such creatures as Greedy Harry Biggs, Dan Pig ('that did make Dan Pig laugh! Ho ho ho!') and the farmer whose horse fell down into a ditch. Later, Saturday mornings were devoted to Uncle Mac and his lovely programme 'Children's Favourites'.

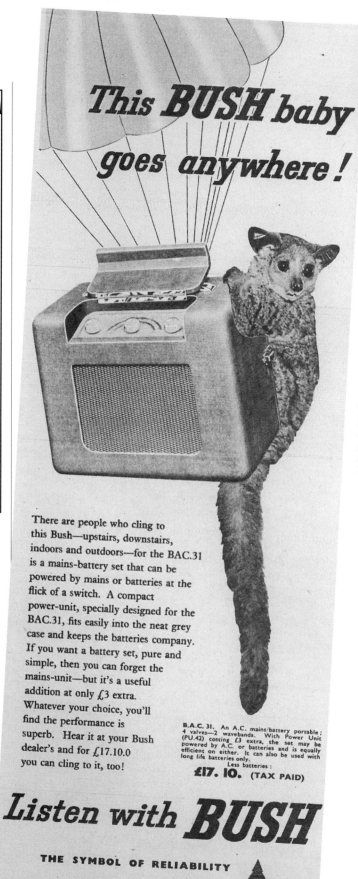

'Listen With Mother' is almost chillingly familiar. It brings back such intense memories. There was always a story, and I remember one in particular. It was about a little girl who has to go shopping for her mother, and she makes up a song about the shopping list. It went like this:
'*Nutmeg, ginger, cinnamon and mace*
Nutmeg, ginger, cinnamon and mace.'
To this day, I recite shopping lists in my mind in exactly the same way. 'Stamps, string, bank, peas.' Make them into groups of four or five, and sing them to myself.

I loved 'Children's Hour'. I used to listen to David Davis, he read all the long children's stories, the serials. The sound of his voice brings back to me all that stuff about dark Sundays – he must have read the stories on Sundays. An amazing voice.

I remember the joy of huddling in front of the fire at night, in a darkened room, and listening to someone to telling you stories such as 'Larry the Lamb' and 'Toytown' out of the huge old Bakelite radio with gold mesh speakers.

DEBORAH MOGGACH (B. 1948)
Pre-central heating, I remember the repeated chorus of 'Close the DOOR!' Chilblains, arctic lavatories and Bronco. The magic of side-indicators popping out of cars. The thrilling luxury of roast chicken and frozen peas! Nobody drinking, except a sherry before Sunday lunch. People whistling and singing in the street. Pervasive dowdiness, and lack of choice, but children only realise that later, and who cared?

I remember the science fiction programme on Sunday nights, 'Journey Into Space' – it scared the hell out of me. I used to stuff things in my ears but I still couldn't miss it, it was the highlight of the week. Absolutely tremendous!

I remember 'The Billy Cotton Band Show' being on the radio, just as Sunday lunch was about to be eaten. 'Wakey wa-a-a-key!' And 'The Goon Show' was something I never missed.

Daddy used to make our radios for us, he made crystal sets with headphones. And 'Saturday Night Theatre' would come on at 8.45 or 9.45 and go on until 10.45, which was really late, and in bed I would listen to a whole lot of really frightening stuff through these headphones, like 'Dr Jekyll and Mr Hyde'. You had to listen through the headphones, because there was no on and off button, the radio was on all the time, only you couldn't hear it unless you had the headphones on. I used to think my father was magic, because of course as soon as you heard him coming you'd take the headphones off and feign sleep. He always knew, miraculously, if I'd had the headphones on. And I only realised ages afterwards that he'd felt the headphones, and if they were warm he'd know I'd just used them.

I loved the Glums on 'Take it From Here':
'*Take it from here*
Don't go away when you can take it from here.'
Dick Bentley and June Whitfield, as Ron and Eth.

At three o'clock on Sundays there was 'Movie Go-Round', with the theme music from *Carousel*, and it was very exciting because you could hear clips from films. The radio was a really big thing. We were radio-dependent. We marked the stages of our days by the radio, just as we do by our watches today. It was always on, never off.

I loved 'Top of the Form'. It was always recorded in a school hall and it was always boys versus girls, and at the end of every round the audience all had to shout 'Come on the boys!' or 'Come on the girls!' And we'd do this in our home; my brother and I would shout 'Come on the boys!' and Mam would shout 'Come on the girls!'

MUSIC AND RECORDS

As the decade progressed, we began hearing and buying records – a magical new sound called rock 'n' roll.

There was something very innocent and wholesome about the songs that were popular in the fifties. 'Sippin' Soda' and 'Singin' the Blues' by Guy Mitchell, 'A Four-legged Friend' by Roy Rogers, 'Secret Love' by Doris Day. Then there was 'The Tennessee Wig Walk', and you could do all the movements to it as you sang along.

I remember the 'Ovaltineys'. Saturday night, I think. And 'Round the Horne'. But we never listened to 'The Goon Show'. The radio was rented, from Radio Rentals. Just like the television was, when we eventually got one in 1958.

We had a family ritual of always listening to 'The Archers'. We used to sit every night and listen. We never listened to 'Mrs Dale's Diary'.

'Educating Archie' with Peter Brough was terrible. Can you imagine, a ventriloquist on radio. Such an absurd concept!

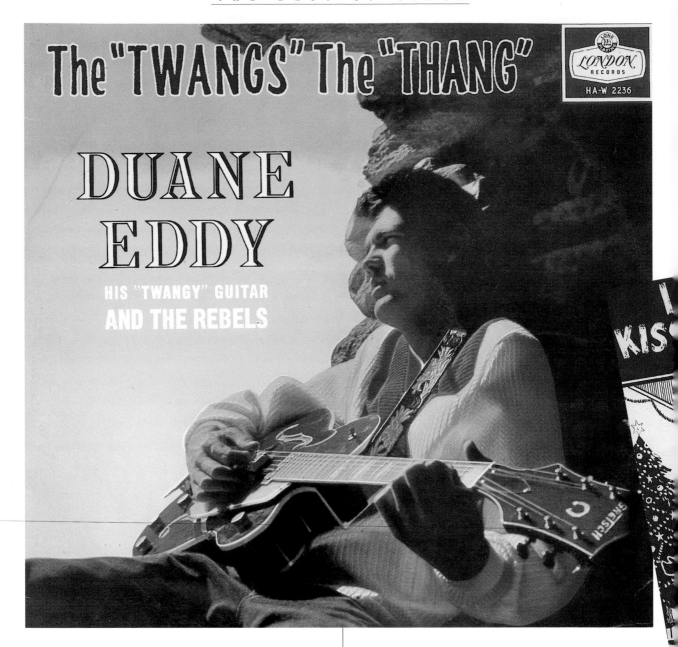

The "TWANGS" The "THANG"

DUANE EDDY
HIS "TWANGY" GUITAR
AND THE REBELS

LONDON RECORDS
HA-W 2236

Records were expensive, and they broke, and they scratched. They cost 7/6, then very quickly 10 bob, when people were only earning about ten quid a week, and when you stood on one or sat on one that was the end of it.

I had an old wind-up record player from my grandmother, with all the old 78s. Things like 'The Laughing Policeman', old music hall stuff. I played them non-stop. My mother hated them and said she'd throw them all out if I didn't stop playing them. I had a bow and arrow, so I took all the records and put them up on the fence and smashed them with my bow and arrow. Everyone was pleased, but that record collection would now be worth hundreds of thousands.

The records that got into me were the records my parents bought. We had Frank Sinatra, *Songs for Swinging Lovers*, with 'Wee Small Hours of the Morning' on it; we had the musicals – *Oklahoma, South Pacific, Kismet, Dancing Years, Kiss Me Kate*. I'm a singer now,

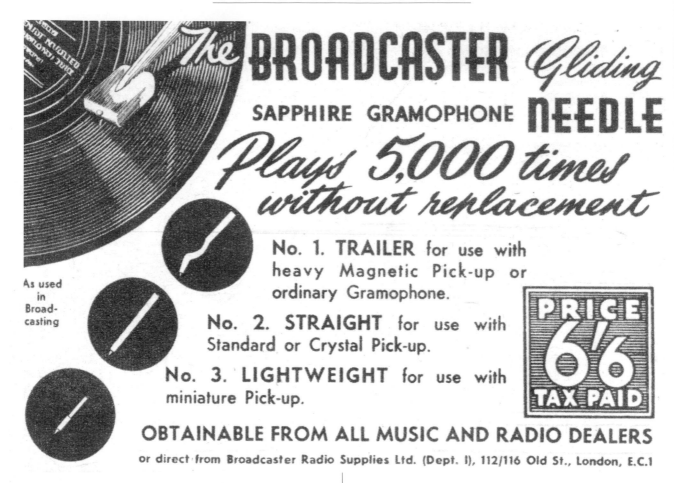

and that's where I get my repertoire from. Frank Sinatra, Lena Horne, Ella Fitzgerald. The one I most remember is Lena Horne's 'Honeysuckle Rose'; on the other side she sang 'Newfangled Tango'. 'Honeysuckle Rose' had sex in every line, a basic swing standard – I just loved it. Ella Fitzgerald's 'Midnight Sun' is just beautiful, you hardly ever hear it nowadays. And there were people like David Whitfield, who until quite recently was performing in pubs in north Wales, and Frankie Lane – an amazing voice. I have an album of his called *That's My Desire*. Of course, I rejected all this music later, in the sixties, but I came back to it.

I was very keen on skiffle when it came out. Lonnie Donegan. Until then I hadn't really been interested in the music played on the radio. We formed a group and played at our school, with a washboard and everything. I got Acker Bilk's autograph, later on.

The first record I ever bought was *Heartbreak Hotel* by Elvis, which came out in 1956. It really was an extraordinary new sound, so thrilling. My parents were appalled.

What we watched

Until television sets became more commonplace in the latter half of the decade, the cinema reigned supreme as the place where we could see new and fantastic worlds. Nothing will ever compete with the sheer glamour of the films and film stars of the 1950s. The very titles of the films – *Carve Her Name With Pride, The Guns of Navarone, High Noon, Seagulls Over Sorrento, Bad Day at Black Rock* **– and the names of the stars – Gary Cooper, Ava Gardner, John Wayne, Jane Russell – still send a shiver down my spine.**

Our parents took us to see *Fantasia* when it first came out. We were too young to appreciate it – I remember enjoying the animal sequences, especially the dancing hippos, but the satyrs were beyond me and most of the music bored me. My sister and I squirmed so much we nearly forced our parents to take us home – but I'm glad we didn't succeed, because I still remember the power of *Night on a Bare Mountain* at the end.

Saturday morning cinema was like another world, which I wasn't usually allowed into. There were hundreds of people there, all shouting and bawling. It was just like a general riot, really. A little man used to come on in front of the curtains and try to do things like hula-hoop competitions. He had no chance. Then we all had to sing the Saturday morning cinema song; then we'd all make terrible animal noises and throw things.

"Not only the film of the week, but perhaps of months..." NEWS OF THE WORLD A film of crackling delight"

Susan Hayward and Kirk Douglas are having FUN in Their Secret Affair

LAUGH HIT OF THE YEAR!

PRESENTED BY WARNER BROS. Written by ROLAND KIBBEE and ALLAN SCOTT Produced by MARTIN RACKIN · MILTON SPERLING Supervising Producer · Directed by H.C. POTTER

NATIONALLY RELEASED from APRIL 28th!

Going to the pictures was just going out, it wasn't about going to see a particular film. It didn't really matter what was showing. It felt grown-up. Mum, Dad and I used to go every Friday evening and sit in the same three seats in the middle of the cinema.

I went to see *Lassie* but I cried so much I had to come out, it was so upsetting.

I loved the epic films of the fifties, and the war films. *The Dam Busters* was my favourite, then later *Ben Hur*.

I thought the Norman Wisdom films were so funny. I think I'd probably squirm with embarrassment if I saw them now, but at the time they were hilarious.

SIR DAVID HARE
(B. 1947)

My Fifties

Dirk Bogarde as Simon Sparrow in *Doctor in the House*: not just the last word in urbanity, but also the last moment in history when people were able to believe that getting the girl (in this case Muriel Pavlow) was the end of the adventure, rather than the beginning.

There was a bit of a competition between local cinemas. You could join the Odeon Club, or the Gaumont Club, show your allegiance and be rewarded. We even had a song, I sang it with Rod Stewart once at a Christmas soccer do. It went
'We come along on a Saturday morning
Greeting everybody with a smile
We come along on a Saturday morning
Knowing that it's all worthwhile
As members of the Odeon Club
We all intend to be
Good citizens when we grow up
And champions of the free.'
We had to sing that before the show started, and the National Anthem.

The first horror films we saw were so terrifying. *The Hound of the Baskervilles*, and *The Pit and the Pendulum*. Would they be as scary today? Probably not, but we weren't used to seeing such things then. It was a new thing for children.

STAGE SHOWS

Theatre outings were a rare treat for most of us in the fifties. Pantomimes were traditional at Christmas, and most towns had a visit from a circus during the year. Then came pop concerts.

We used to go to Richmond Theatre, and the theatre in town. We also used to go and see Billy Smart's Circus at Olympia, and that was really exciting. It was tenpence, and we took the 267 from the top of the road all the way to Olympia. The flea circus was the best.

CHU CHIN CHOW ON ICE

The world-famous musical tale of the East, told in the modern manner

EMPIRE POOL WEMBLEY

COSY NOOK - NEWQUA

Proprietors   NEWQUAY URBAN DISTRICT COUNCIL
Lessees
Manager   HEDLEY CLAXTON PRODUCTIONS LTD.
Telephone   RONNIE MASTERS
                     NEWQUAY 3365

Hedley Claxton presents

GAY·TIME

A SPARKLING SUMMER SHOW

ROLLETT

SOUVENIR PROGRAMME

SIXPENCE

The amateur dramatic society in the village put on lots of plays, nearly all farces – Brian Rix-type stuff. *The Cuckoo's Nest* or something like that was one. That's where my Uncle Horace met my Auntie Margaret. I imagine that most of them were ghastly, but I was no judge as a child.

On our annual holidays in Scarborough we'd go to the rep shows and watch people like Ken Dodd. Always a bit of a laugh.

The annual Christmas pantomime was a real treat. I remember one where we children had to call out 'I'm as daft as a brush!' all the time. Great fun!

By the end of the fifties my friends and I were going to see pop singers on stage: Wee Willie Harris, Eddie Cochrane, and Jerry Lee Lewis.

"You and your MacDonald Hobley! Are we eloping or are we not?"

TELEVISION

The coming of the television set into nearly every household in the land was undoubtedly the biggest and most influential social phenomenon of the decade. It changed our lives.

My father actually made our first television set, in the early fifties. I remember playing out in the garden with my sister and being called in because the television was working. So we rushed inside, really excited, and drew the curtains, and Daddy turned the television on, and instead of a picture there was one of those green dots you used to get in the middle of the set. That was it. We were bitterly disappointed.

We loved all the children's programmes of the fifties. We started with 'Watch With Mother': Rag, Tag and Bobtail, Muffin the Mule, The Flowerpot Men, Andy Pandy, The Woodentops – who could ever forget the two children dancing and prancing around singing 'Peas for dinner! Peas for dinner!' rapturously – then graduated to 'Crackerjack' and the Huw Wheldon science programmes. Great stuff. You got a cabbage to carry on 'Crackerjack' if you got a question wrong, and people ended up in such straits!

The whole neighbourhood used to congregate in the front room of the one household in the street to have television in the mid-fifties. We'd watch 'Children's Hour'. One girl's mother always came with her and drove the rest of us batty, because being used to radio she'd describe everything that was happening on screen, loudly, all the time, as if we couldn't see it for ourselves.

The first programme I remember watching and enjoying is 'Lost in Space'. But it frightened me. It was a serial. I had to have the light left on when I went to bed after that was on.

Sylvia Peters was so glamorous and wonderful, wearing her evening dresses. 'Good evening, viewers.' She had a perfect heart-shaped face. Gilbert Harding, on the other hand, was so gruff.

On Sundays there was a programme called 'All Your Own' with Huw Wheldon, and children who had made cathedrals out of matchsticks would come on and show us how clever they were. The child we despised most was a girl with bunches in her hair who did Irish dancing with her hands by her side. We found that so annoying. Huw Wheldon would thank everyone at the end and say that he hoped we'd watch next week the programme that was 'well and truly, all your own'.

I hated 'The Brains Trust'. My parents and uncle all used to sit and watch this, so I did too, and I just didn't understand it. I suppose it was like current affairs programmes now.

Eamon Andrews seemed to be in every television programme broadcast during the 1950s: 'What's My Line?', 'Crackerjack', and about a hundred more. He was a more familiar figure than most of my far-flung relatives – a part of the family, despite the Irish accent.

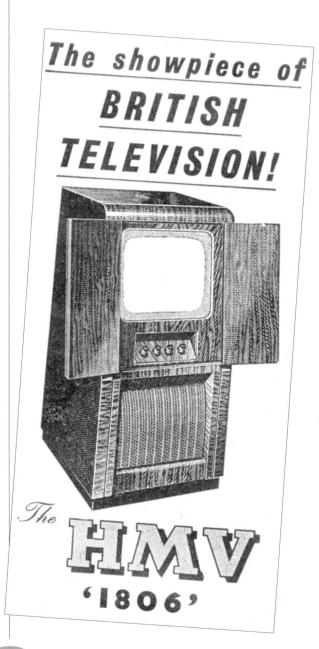

The showpiece of **BRITISH TELEVISION!**

The **HMV** '1806'

Postscript: the end of the age of innocence

GROWING UP

By the end of the fifties our teenage years were on us, or loomed large, and things were never to be the same again. The unprecedented freedom and largesse we had enjoyed as children led to us being the first generation to really have a 'teenage'. And we certainly made the most of it.

My friends were all a year older than me so when I was eleven they all had their Louis heels and make-up, and I couldn't have those things. Then I began to paint my nails because my sister did, and shave my legs because my sister did, and before I knew it I was a teenager.

I always played with the neighbourhood boys, not girls, because I found them more interesting. I wanted to kick footballs and climb trees. Then one day when I was about eleven I painted my nails, because I'd seen my sister do it, and the boys turned on me nastily. They ganged up on me in the shed, held me down and cut all my nails off with a pair of clippers. Tomboys weren't allowed to become girls. Of course, later they did allow me to become a girl, once they realized what it was all about.

My mother let me into the Big Secret by giving me a little book one day when I was eleven. It was in a brown envelope and it came, I noticed, from *Woman*, the magazine she read.

Intriguing. She told me to read it and then come and ask her anything I did not understand. The trouble was that I did not understand a word of it. What I read was all about ashes: the body of a woman cleaning out its own ashes once a month, and not to be frightened by it as it was a purifying process. I failed to see the word 'blood' because I'd already got the image of ashes – as we cleaned the grate out every day – lodged firmly in my mind.

In our day we were more embarrassed by periods than anything else. It would have been much easier if we could have discussed it with each other. In the days of the sanitary towel, which you carried to school at the bottom of your satchel in a crumpled brown paper bag so it got squashed beneath homework and littered with pencil shavings and ink stains, you were instructed to burn them in the incinerator rather than flush them away. There can be no more irrational and silly fear than waiting in the toilet cubicle till the last voice had gone so I could dash out and tip the dreaded thing into the incinerator when no one was looking.

My friend and I each had a gang, we were top girls at our primary school. Then I went to her birthday party and we had to play 'Postman's Knock', which involved going outside the room and kissing a boy in the hall. I found this quite frightening. So was 'Forfeits' – I always worried that this would involve removing some item of clothing. And I was right, it usually did.

Sex was never, ever mentioned when I was a child. Never. It was evil, dirty, never to be discussed. So I spent my time playing outdoors, never thinking about girls until I was about sixteen. I was just a happy, sports-mad kid.

In the late fifties, when I was 11 or 12 and my sister a year older, we started going to parties with the local kids and playing games like 'Spin the Bottle' and 'Postman's Knock', and ending up with the lights switched off and everyone coupled off – just for 'necking', nothing more. One time we both got home a little flushed and a little worried about what our parents would say, but all those trivial worries were swept away in a tidal wave of horror when we learnt on arrival that our dog had been run over that night. It put all that stuff into perspective for us.

feminine 'know-how'

Make yourself *extra* lovely at "those certain times". With gay fresh flowers pinned in your hair, you'll look in party mood— and *feel* it ! And with the perfect sanitary protection of MODESS, you'll enjoy every minute of the dance !

Modess
Softer...Safer...Streamlined...

A *Johnson & Johnson* product.

I remember trying to scream at the pop stars – well, we did scream. My school beret went up in the air during one of the Elvis films, and was never seen again. And dancing in the aisles. *Loving You* was my favourite film for ages. And *Jailhouse Rock*.

FIRST LOVE
As ever, first love was agony and ecstasy.

The first date I ever had was in 1959. I was 12, and we went to see *The World, the Flesh and the Devil,* an X-rated film. After saying hello we didn't exchange another word all evening, not even when I fell down the stairs twice coming out of the cinema because of the ridiculous high heels I was wearing. We never went out together again.

A boy called Martin used to walk me home from the swimming baths every Thursday night, and he'd stop in the park and say, 'Shall we?', meaning kiss.

I received my first Valentine card in 1959, when I was 11. It had inside a handwritten verse:
'I loved you then,
I love you still,
But darling, no more –
I never will.'
Well, he never did, because to this day I don't know who sent it, or why, or what exactly it meant.

I met my first love at the church youth club. That was the best thing about going to Sunday School: eventually, it turned into the youth club, and you met boys and started snogging.

I remember the girls' changing rooms with girls smearing on lipstick and puffing up their hair, backcombing it then spraying it with awful-smelling hairspray.

I was gripped by people kissing on television. It was a fascination linked with horror. I wondered for many years whether, to be kissed, the woman had to put her arms up loosely around the man's neck and accept his head coming down on hers while she leaned backwards.

My first boyfriend was a terrible *poseur* who dressed like a Teddy boy but was really very wimpish and shy. He wore drainpipe trousers and fluorescent socks and a jacket with a velvet collar. I tried to dress like his moll but my heart wasn't really in it – and I was too young, anyway.

BAD HABITS
Our major bad habit was smoking.

My friend Ann began smoking when she was about ten. We'd scour the gutters of our home town, looking for dumpers. Sometimes you'd get half an inch, or even an inch, of unsmoked cigarette. I didn't smoke myself, but I aided and abetted her.

I began smoking when I was about nine or ten. In those days you could buy single cigarettes, Woodbines or Senior Service, from the corner shops, no questions asked. I used to put bits of cotton wool in my boxes of matches so they didn't rattle when I was at home. My clothes and hair must have smelt of tobacco, but my parents didn't seem to notice. Of course, they both smoked too.

All of a sudden there were lots of teenage dances. They all had a last waltz, and it was terribly important to dance the last waltz with the right boy.

There was a dance hall my sister and I started going to at a really early age, pre-teen, towards the end of the fifties. The boys there almost jitterbugged rather than jived, in trousers that flapped around their legs. It was an incredibly sexy place, looking back.

At some stage, we turned into scheming little harridans, wearing high heels and bright red lipstick and striking poses wherever we could. But it was all still very innocent – we had no real idea of the consequences of what we were doing. That came later.

I remember the first time I got dressed especially to impress a boy at the church youth club. This involved wearing an awful dress that had no sleeves and layers of purple frills, and I had to buy a purple velvet headband to match. Because I had to get him. Lots of backcombing the hair, and lots of lacquer. It didn't work. He didn't fancy me at all.

On the way back from the local dance hall – we were allowed to go there in the late fifties, even though we were barely into our teens – the boys would end up scrawling filthy drawings on the garage doors in the laneways. An early form of graffiti.

Brave new world

There was such a feeling of 'Brave New World' about the fifties. Everything seemed wonderfully clean and fresh and bright and new. We were clean and healthy, clothes were clean, mothers wore bright red lipstick.

We were at the beginning of the push to get as many boys and girls as possible into the redbrick universities. Boys and girls from working-class homes, with parents who had no academic aspirations, were now seeing themselves as university fodder. Girls whose mothers had never imagined them as anything more than secretaries were being caught up in the tide of enthusiasm.

We also wanted to have fun. We did not want to be like the prefects of two or three years ahead — they seemed drab and boring, girls who had sacrificed their lives to getting on at school. We had this notion that it was possible for us to be clever, witty and bad, and still do well at school.

We were definitely brought up in the best of times. Even twenty years earlier, I'd have ended up as a drudge; fifty years earlier, I'd have been a tweenie. The post-war years opened countless doors for us children of Britain, and I like to think that we're still aware of that, still appreciate what a charmed life we've led.